Happy Chubby Dogs

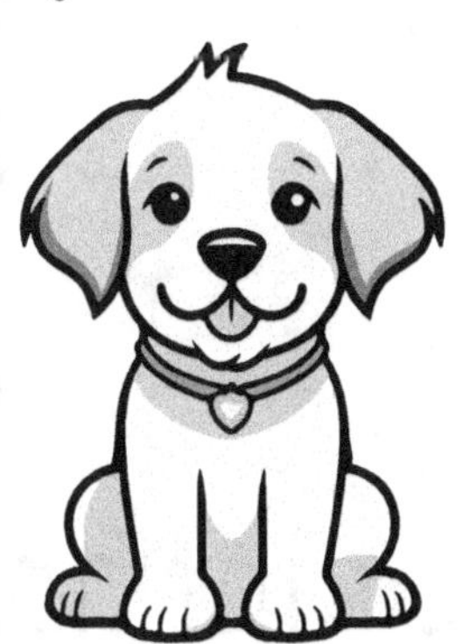

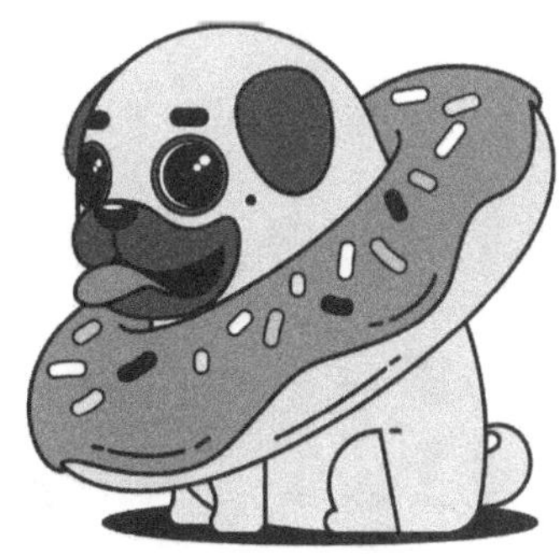

Thank you for being a part of this incredible journey with us. Together, we can inspire a lifelong love for reading and ignite the imagination of young dreamers everywhere.

Your Thoughts Matter! Share Your Book Review Today

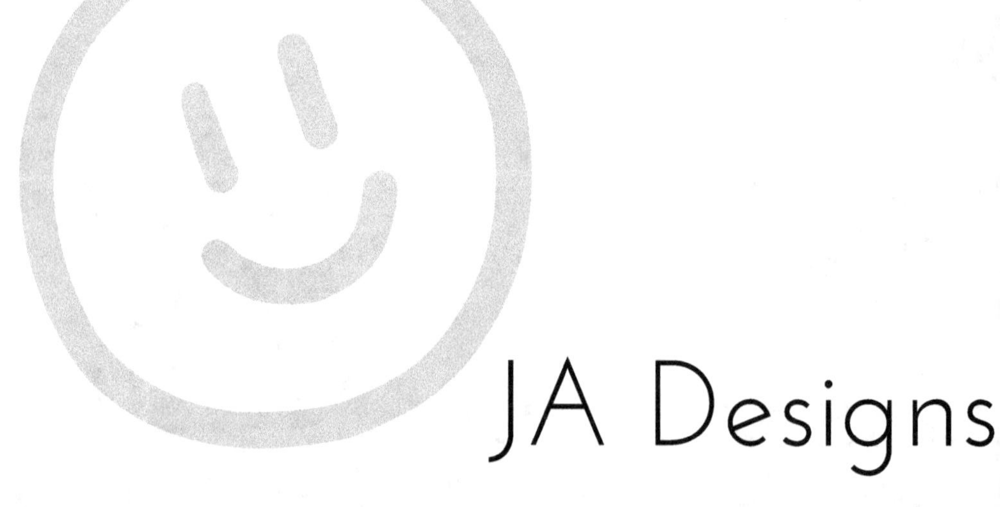

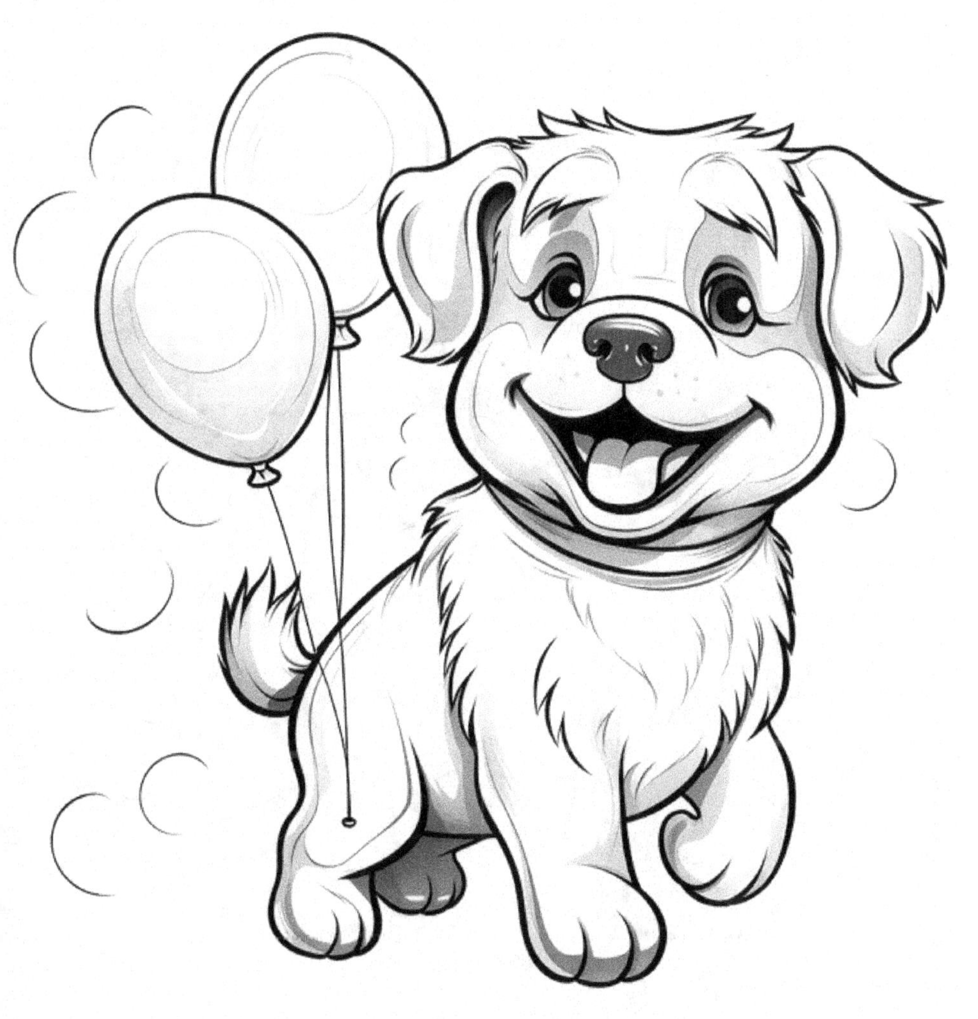

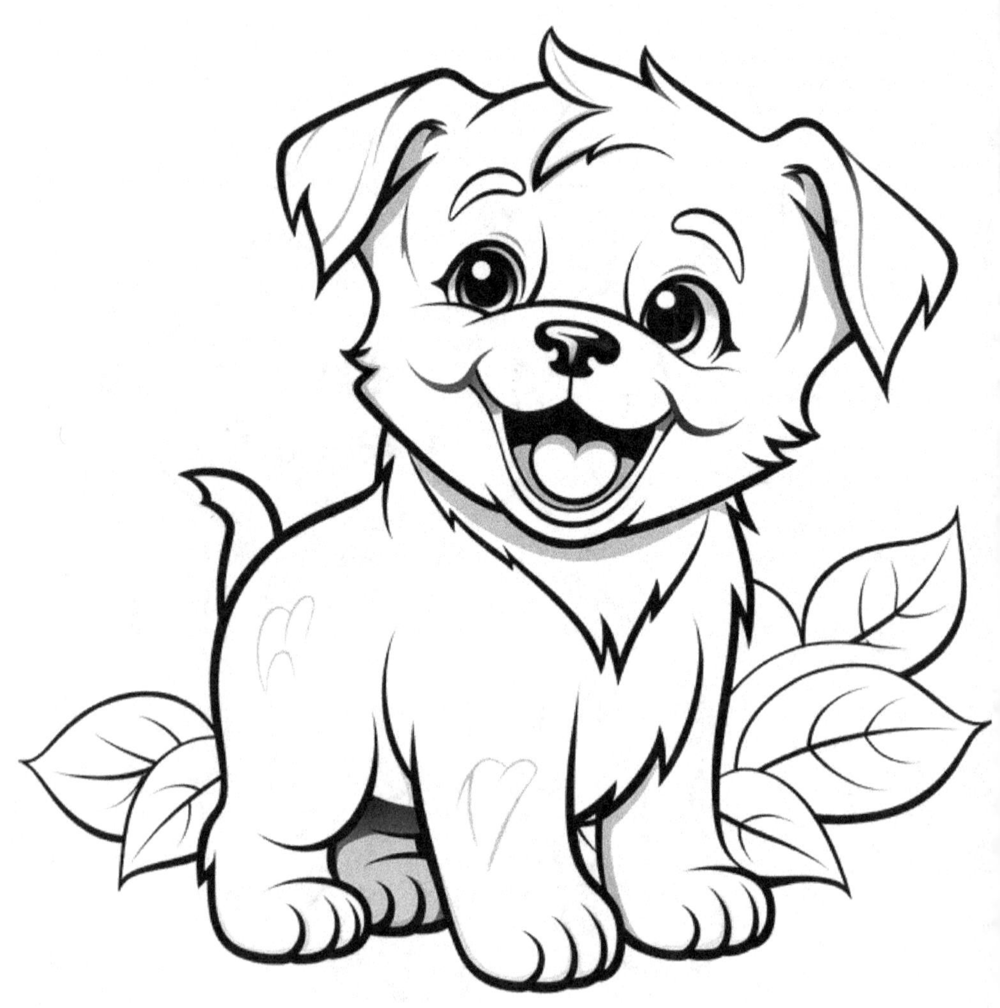

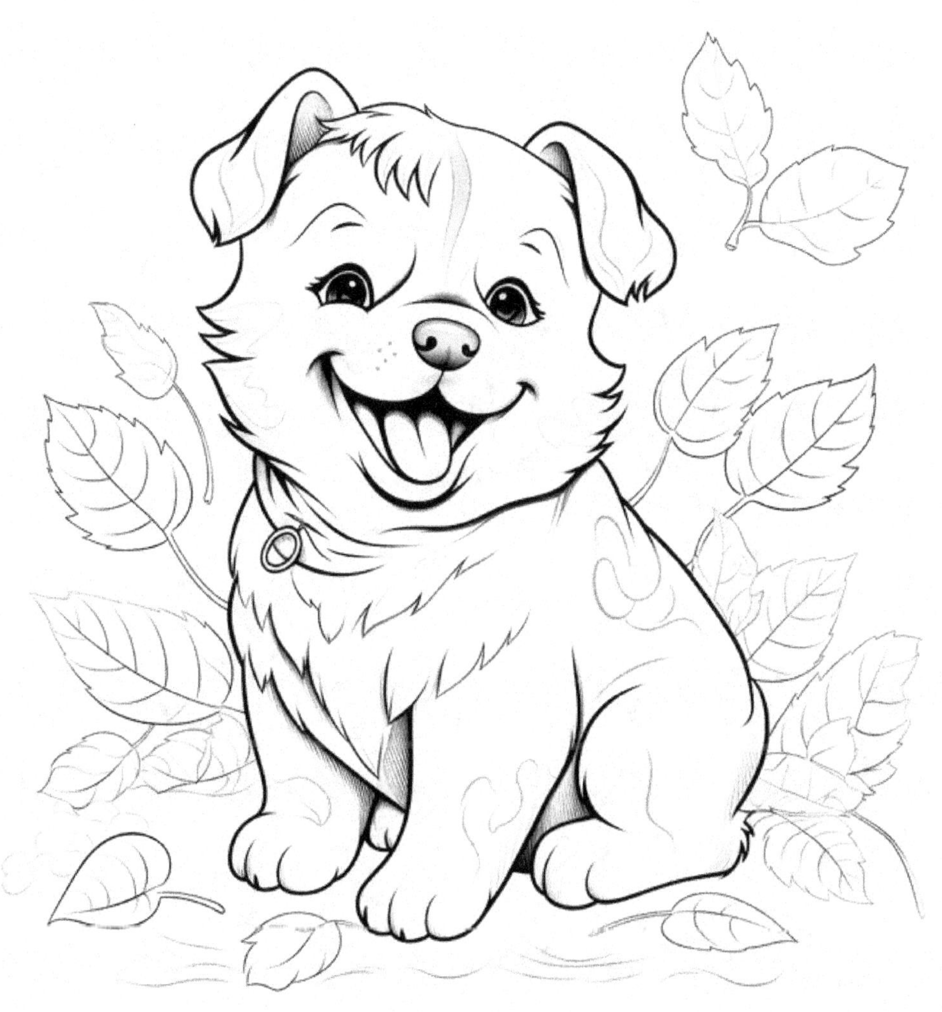

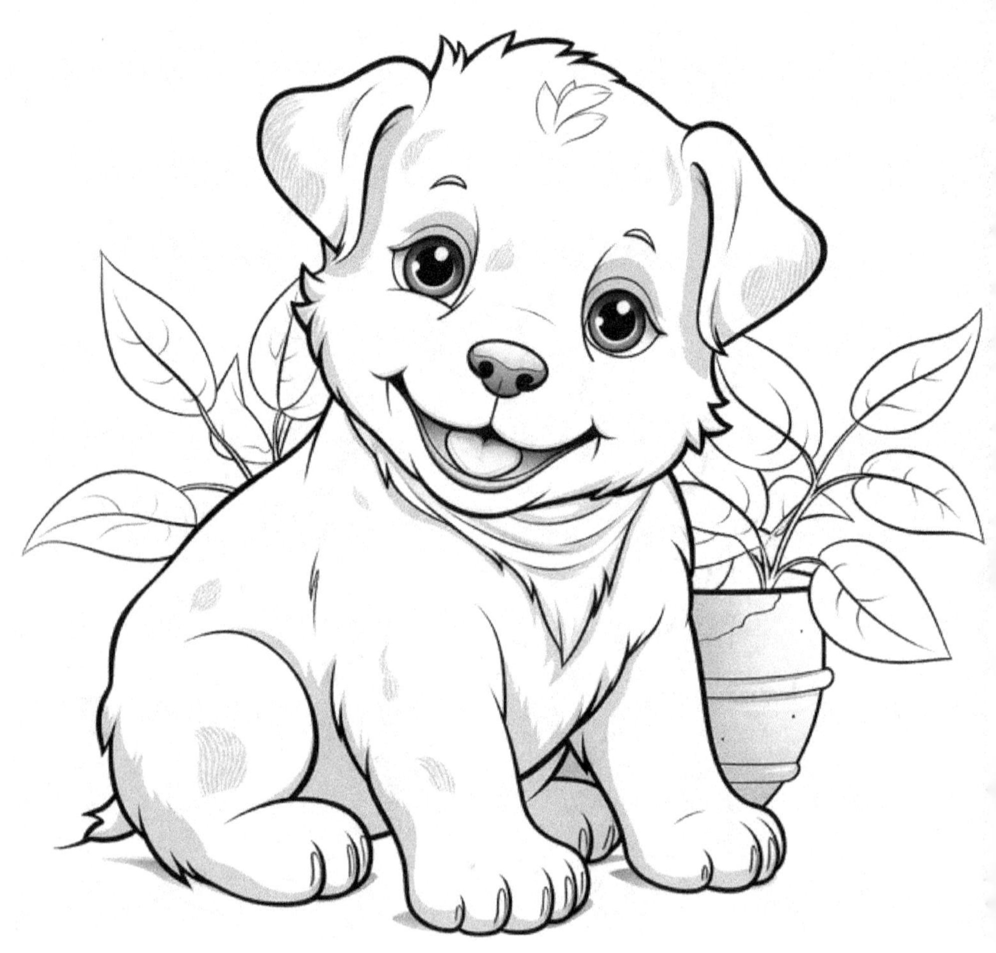

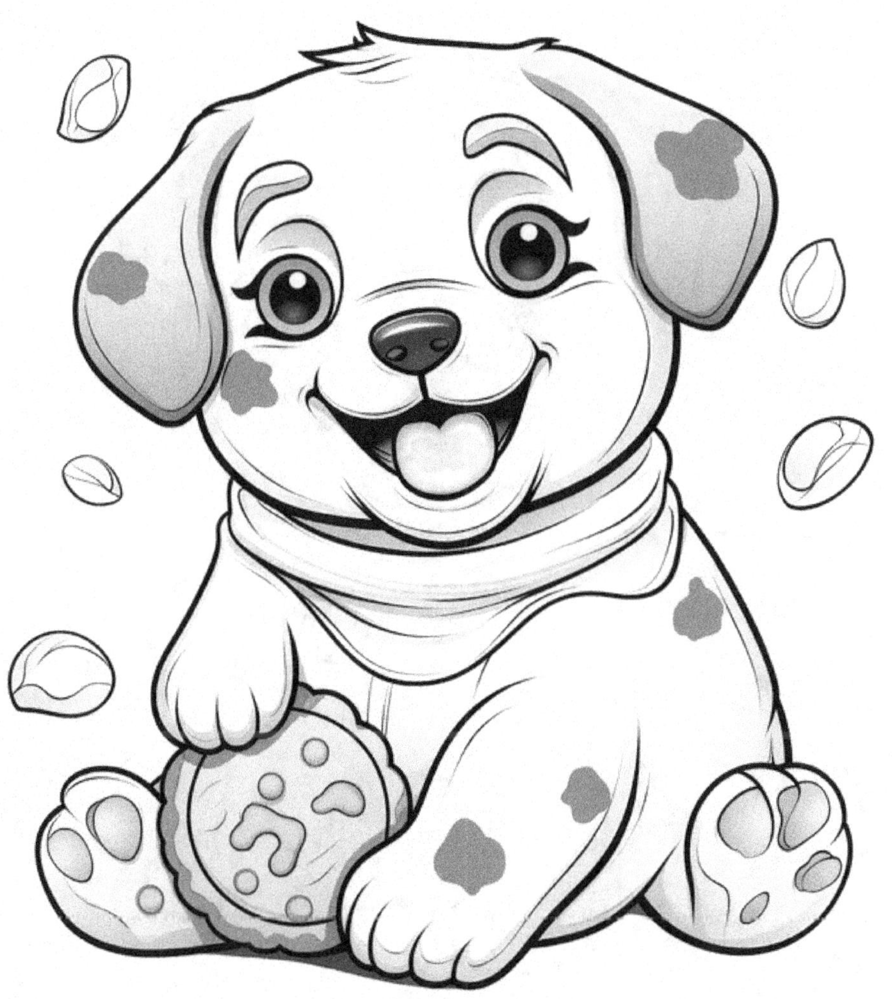

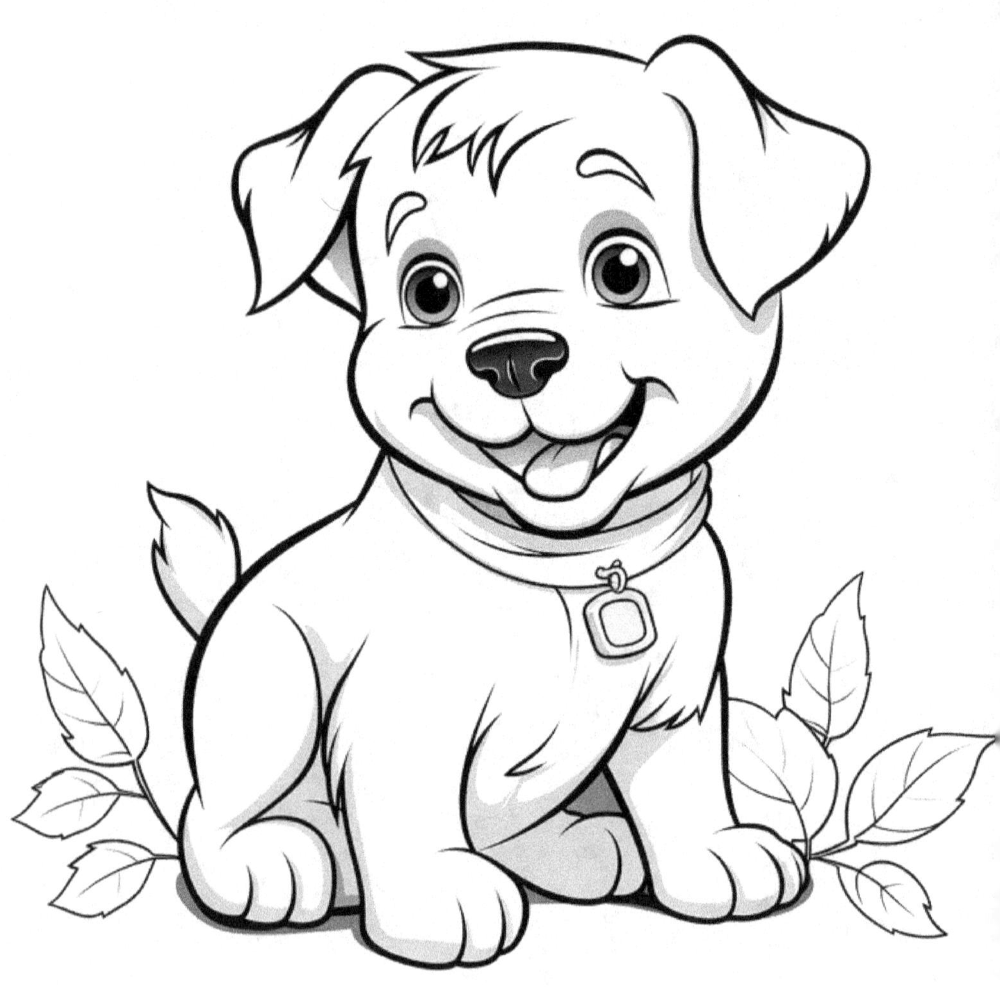

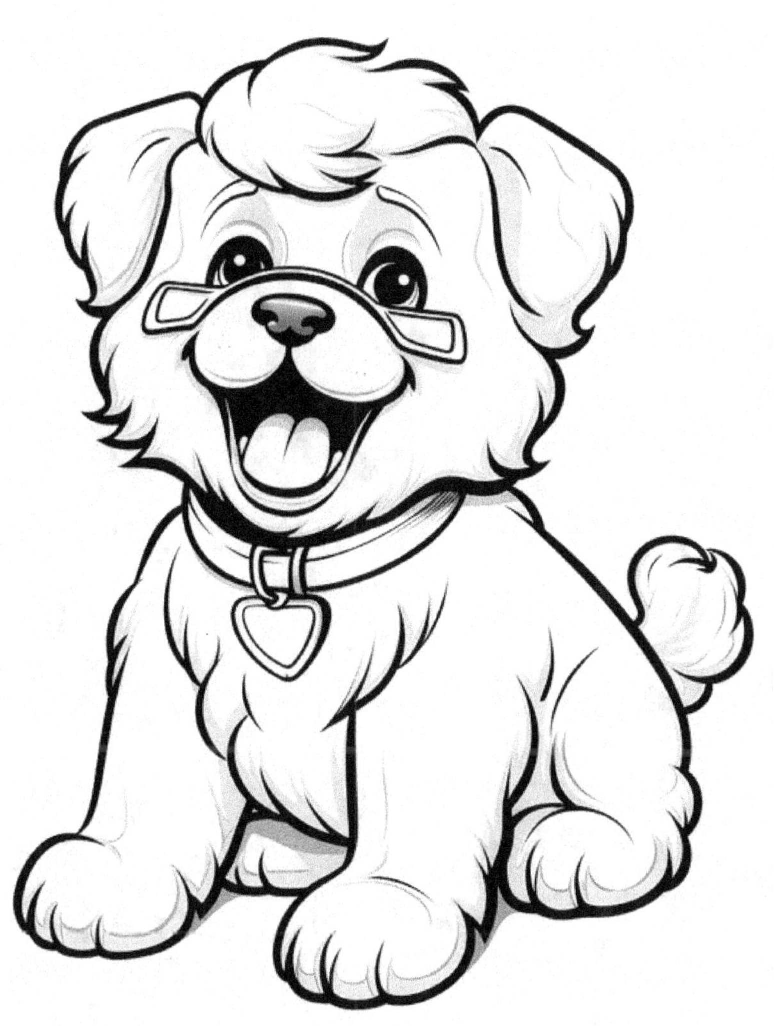

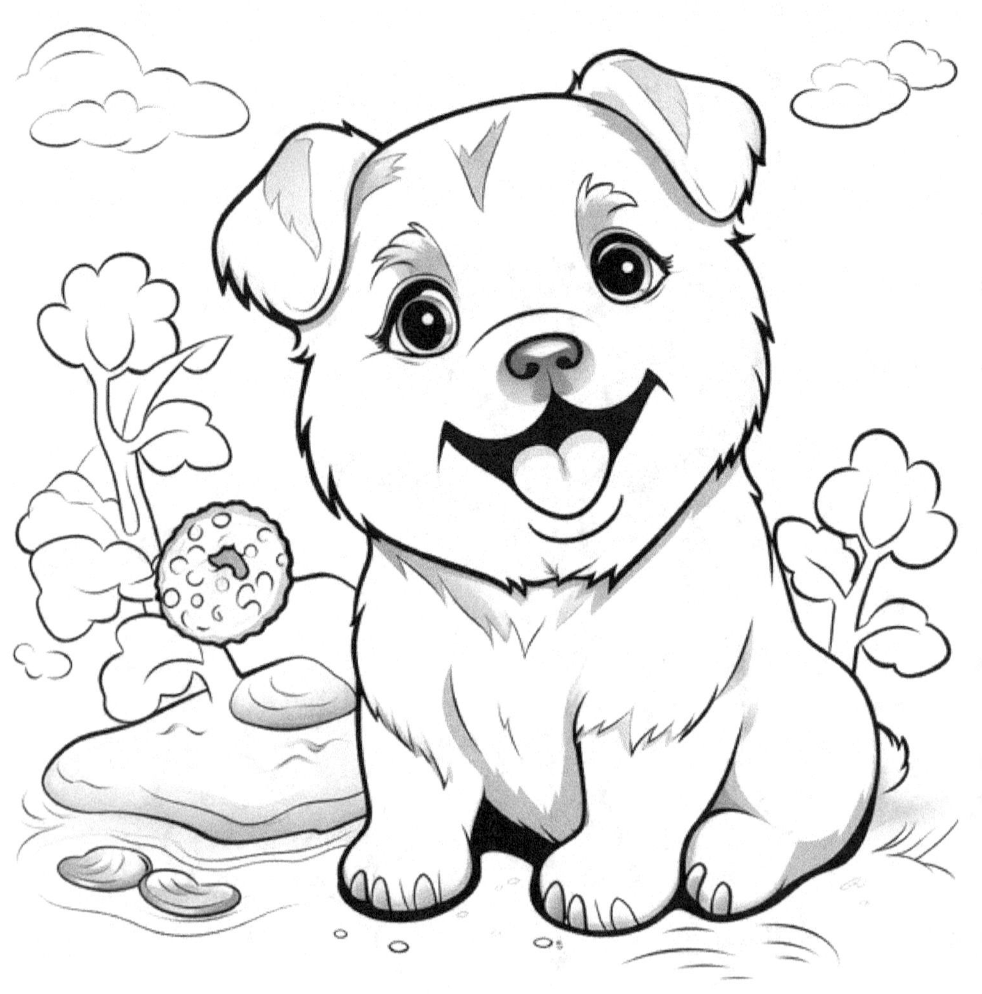

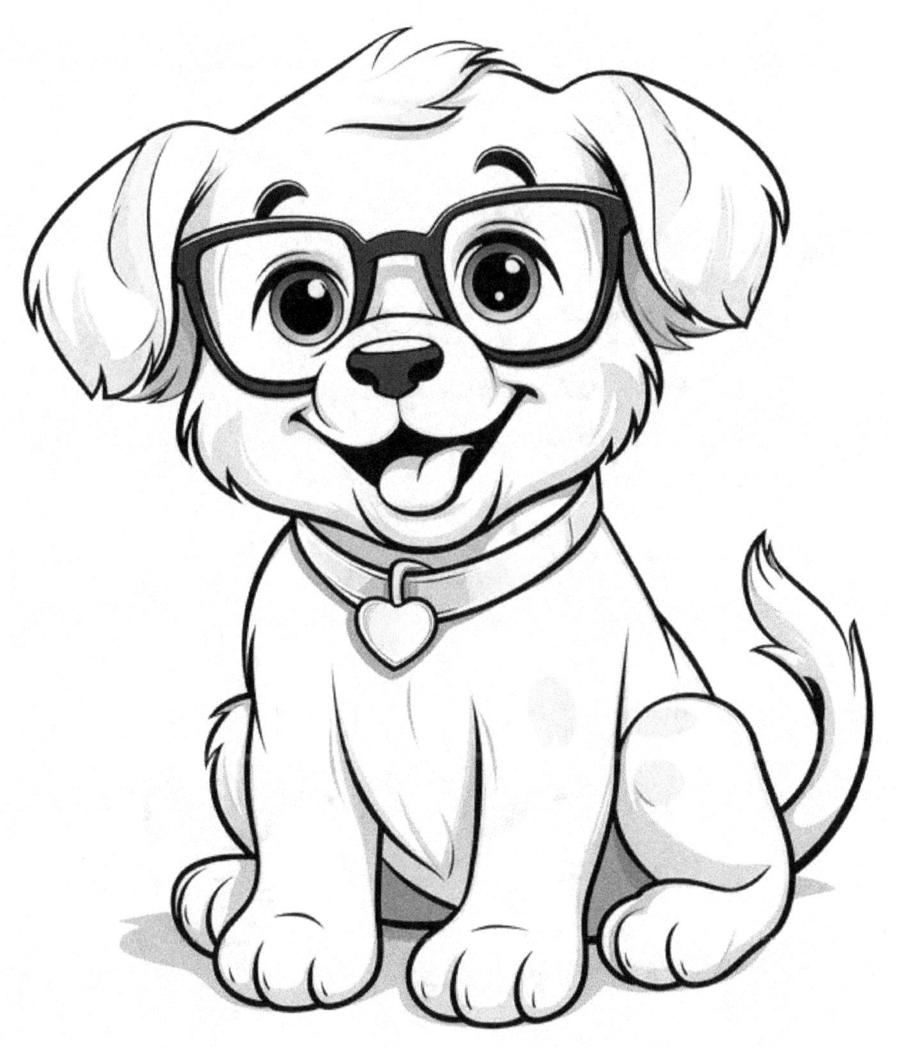

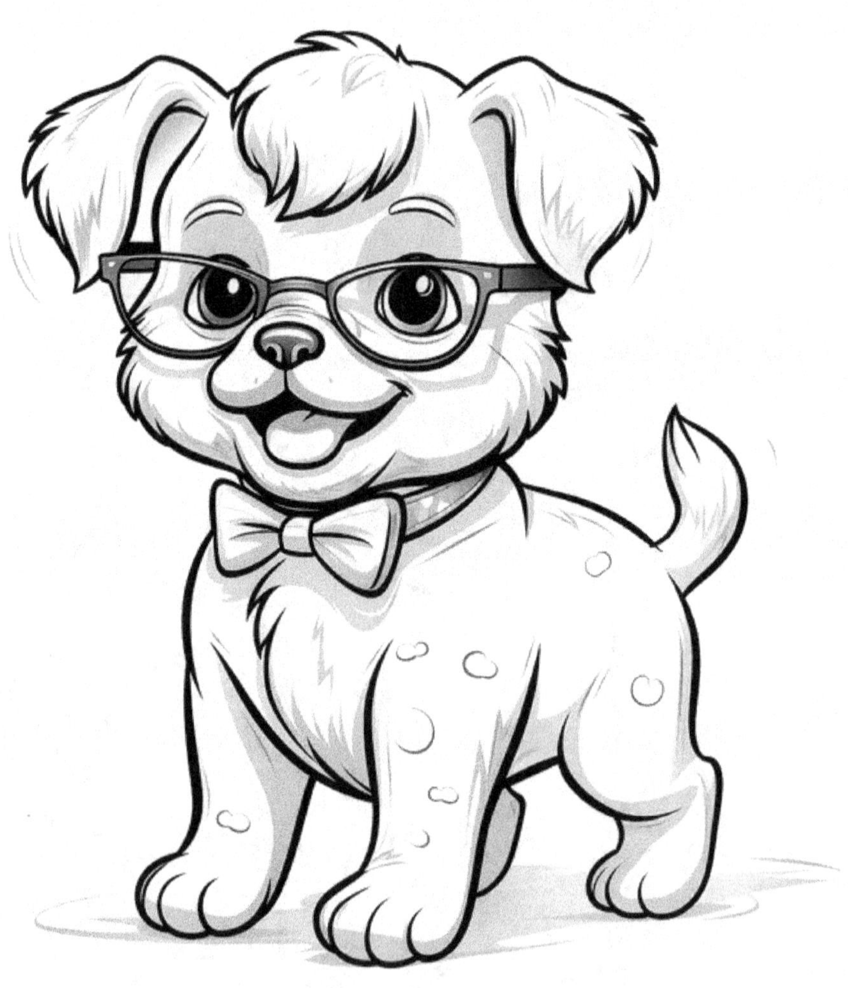

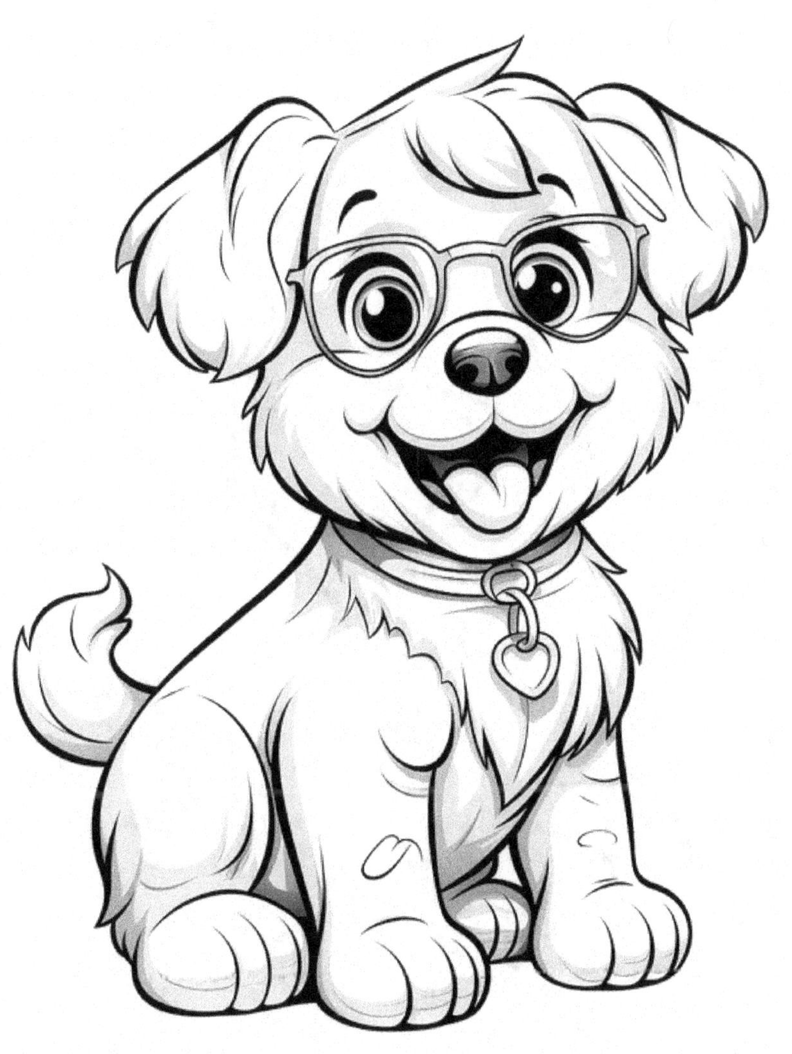

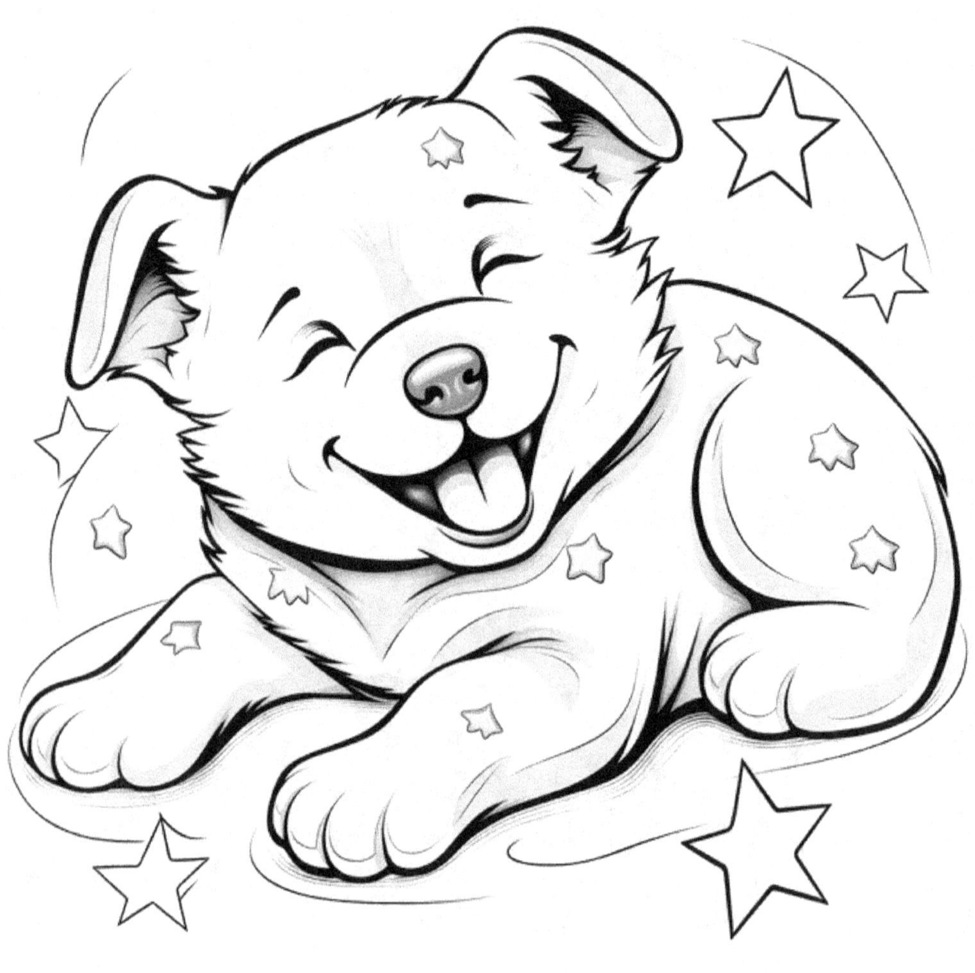

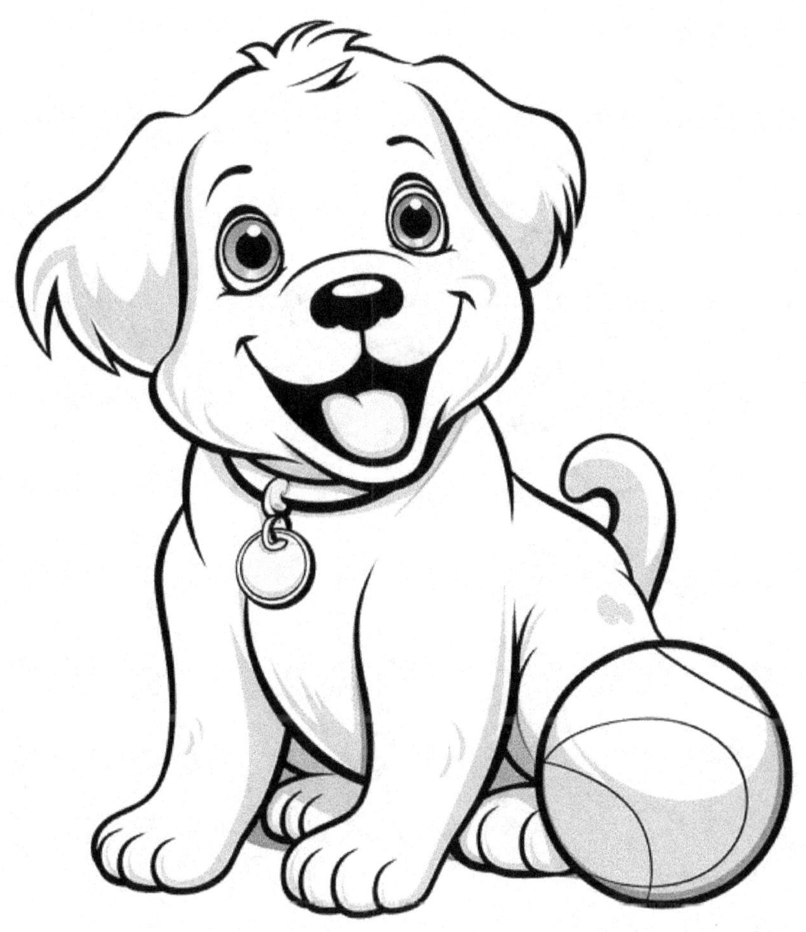

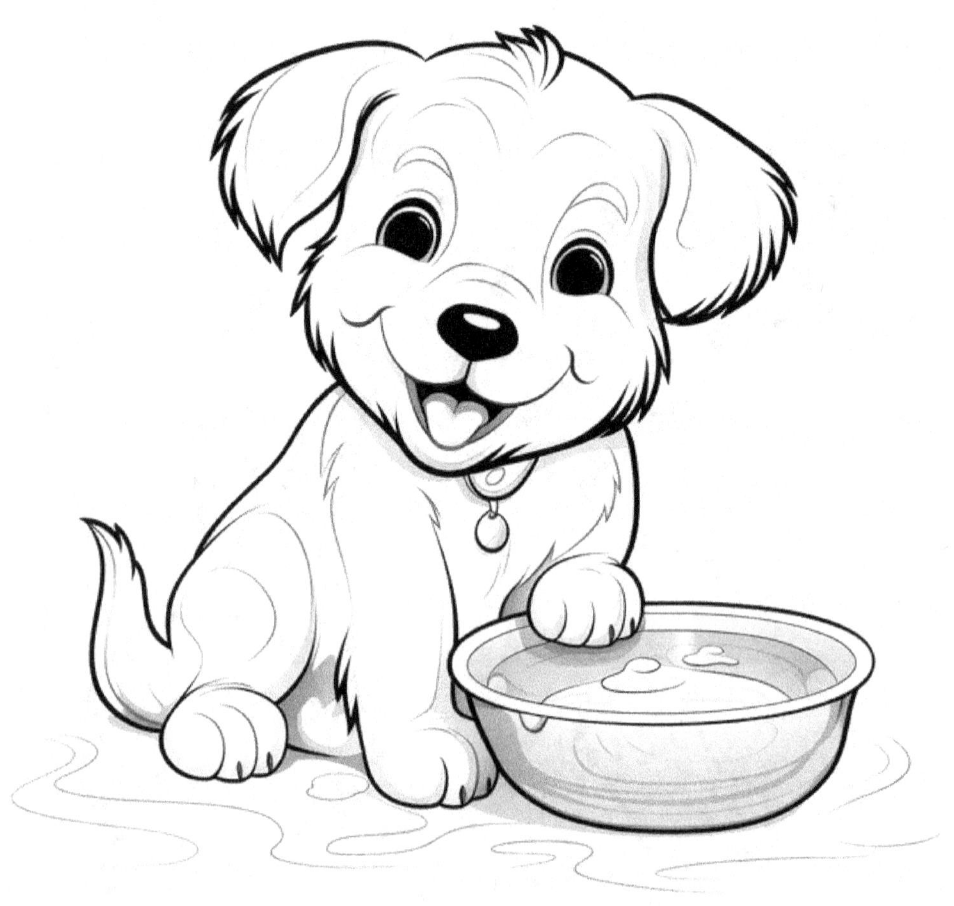

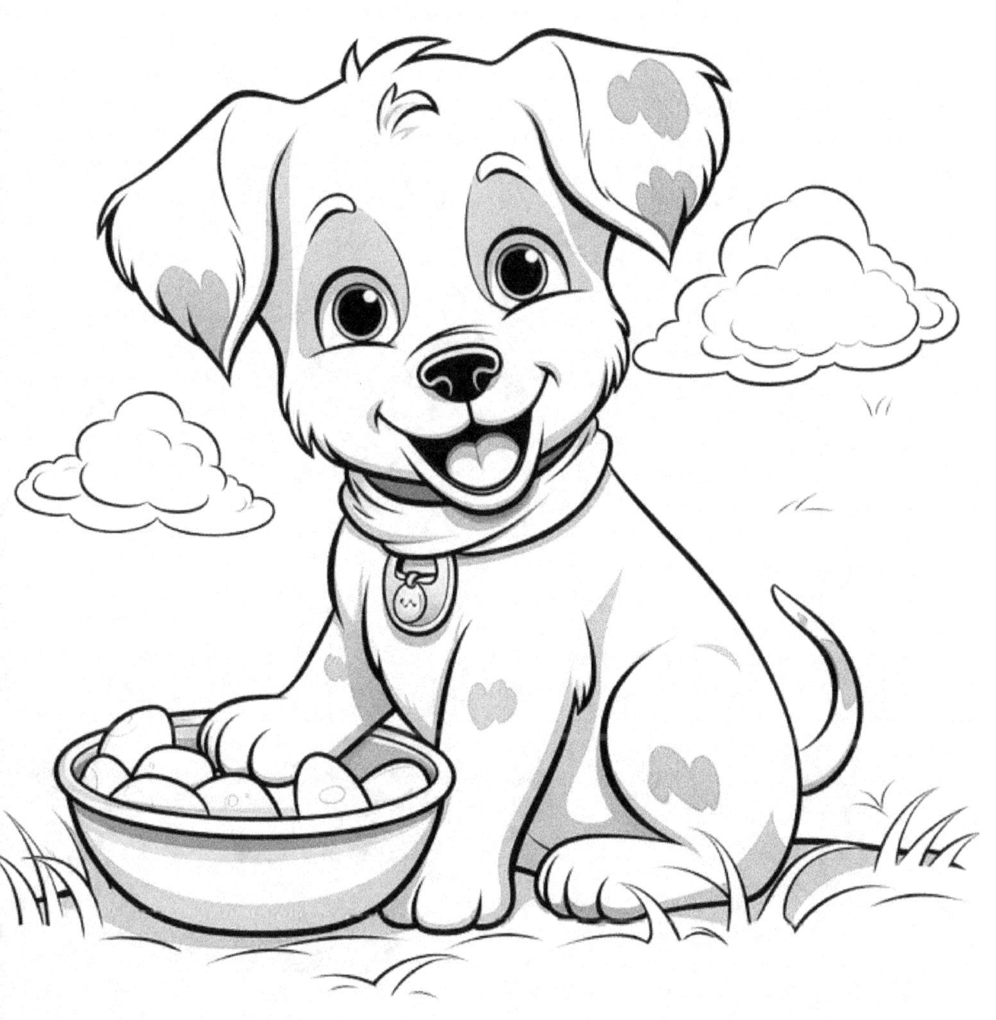

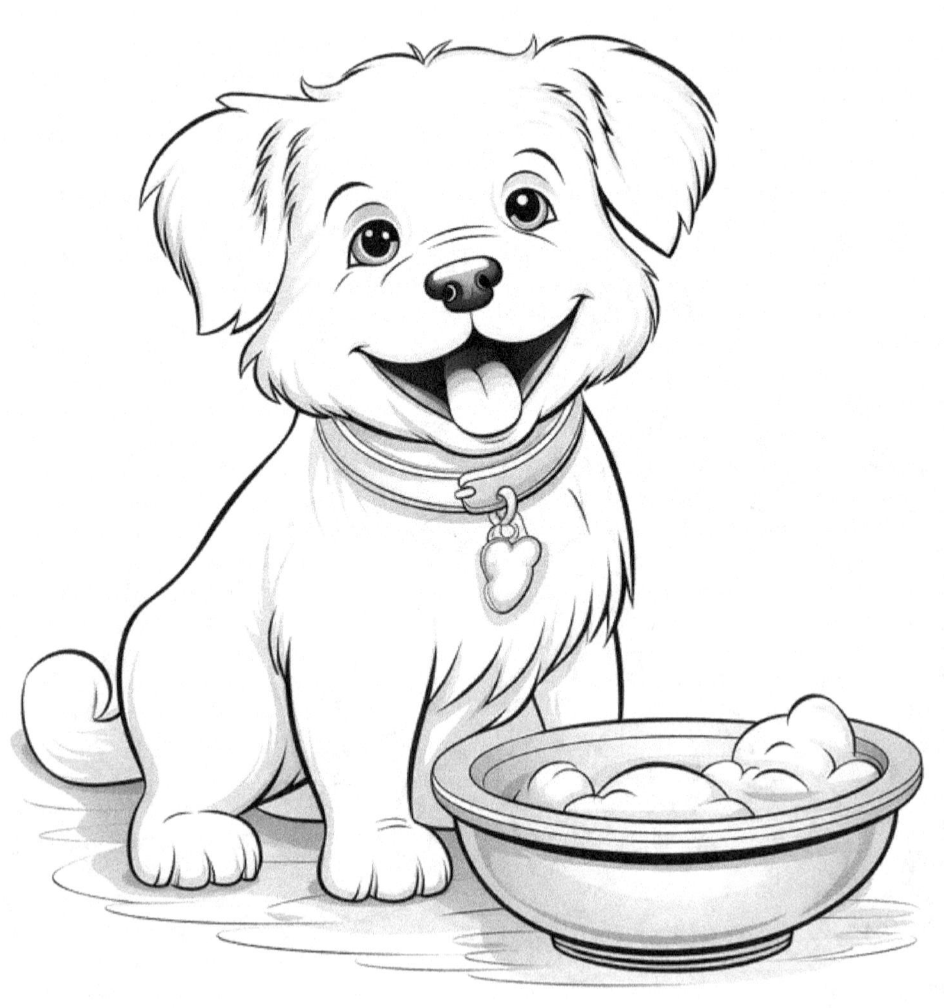

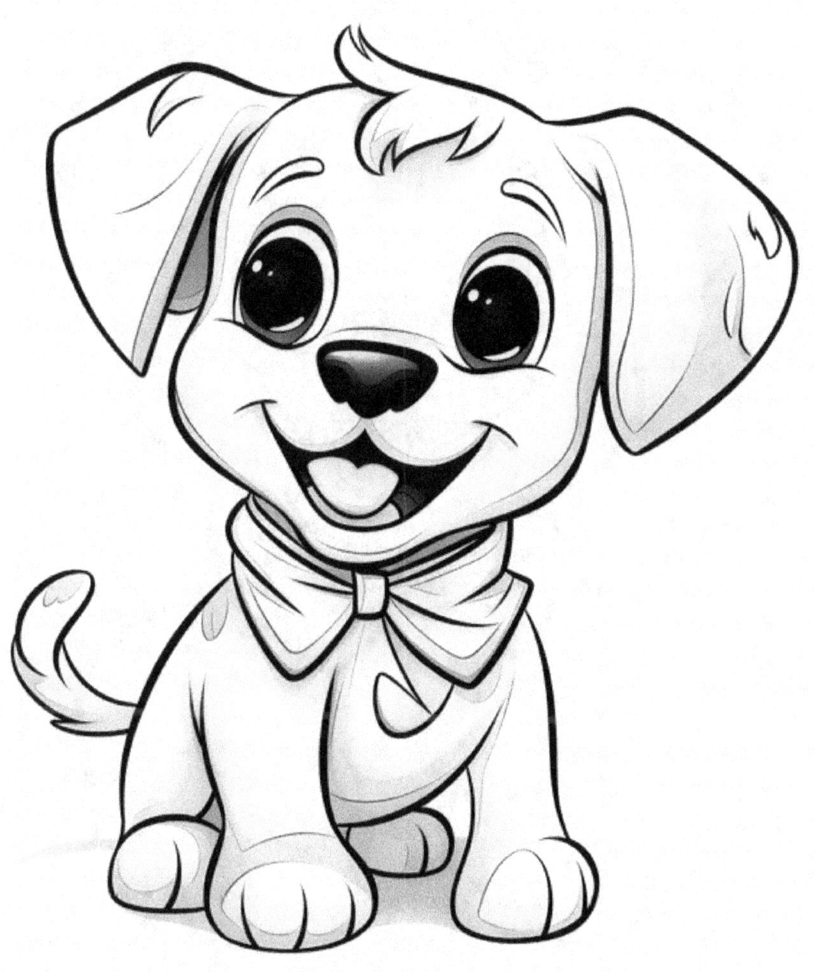

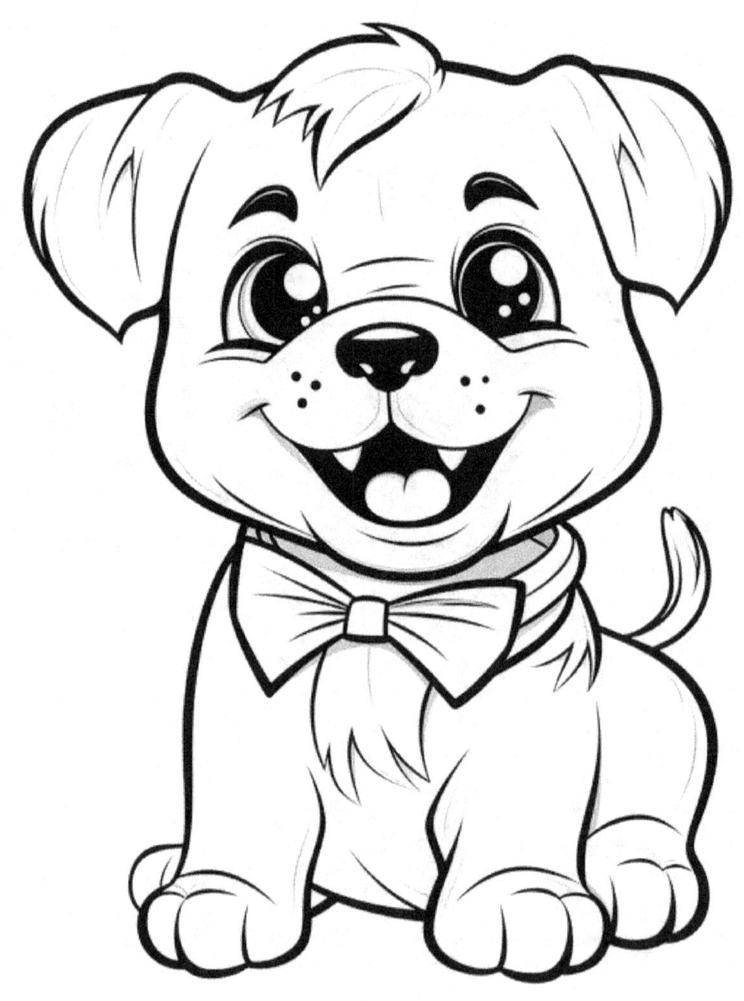

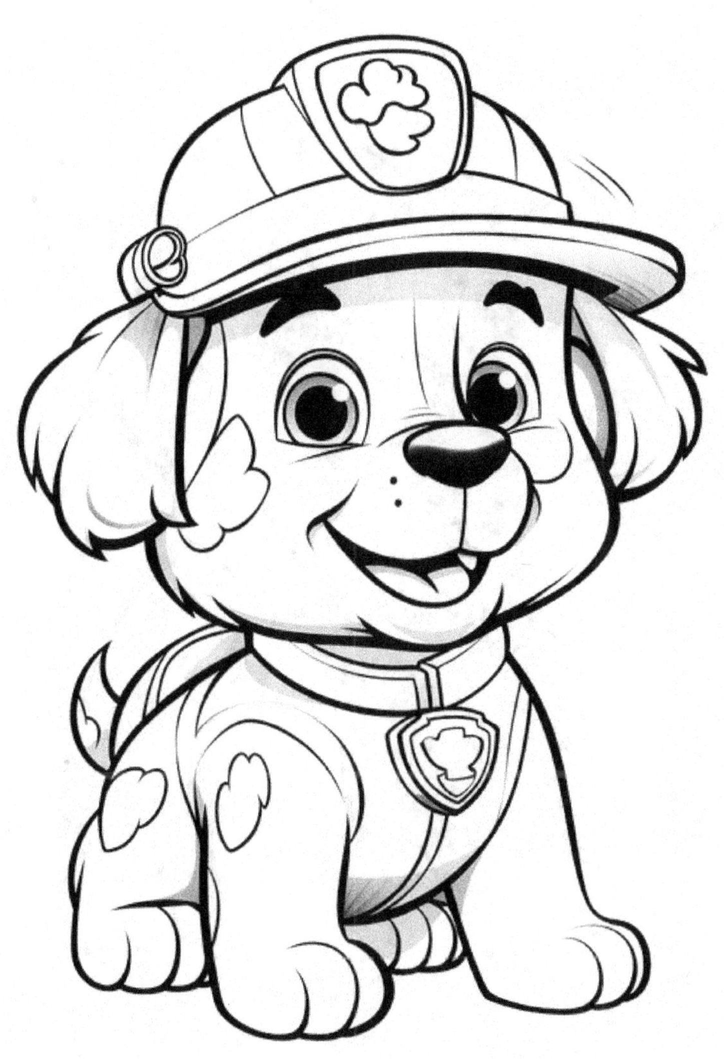

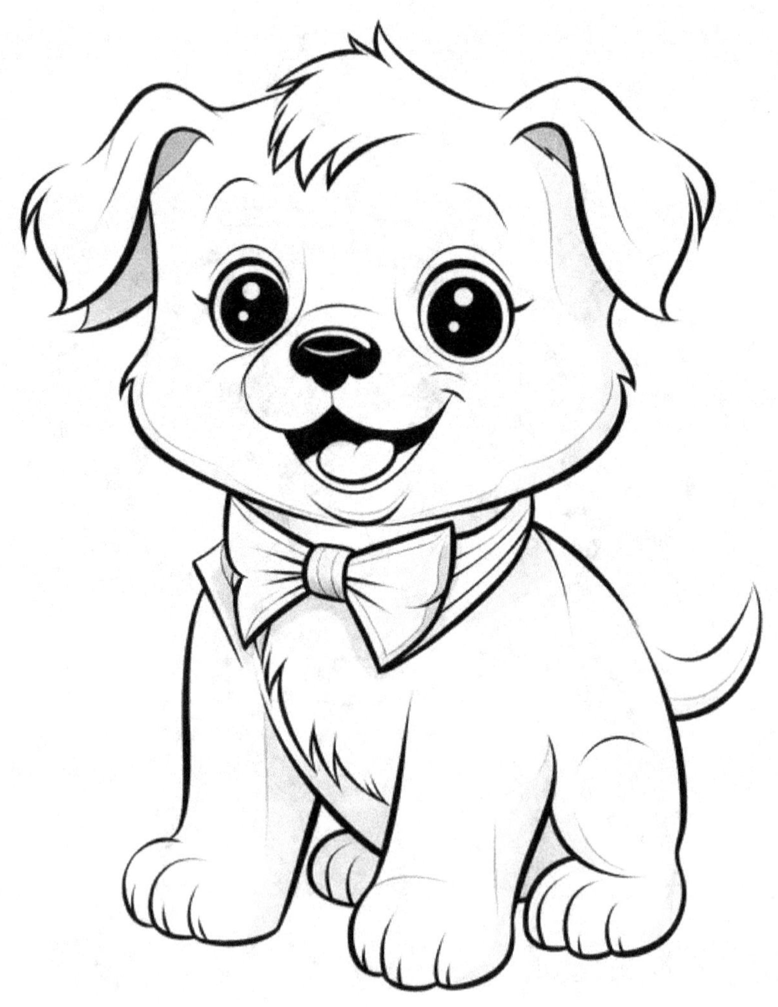

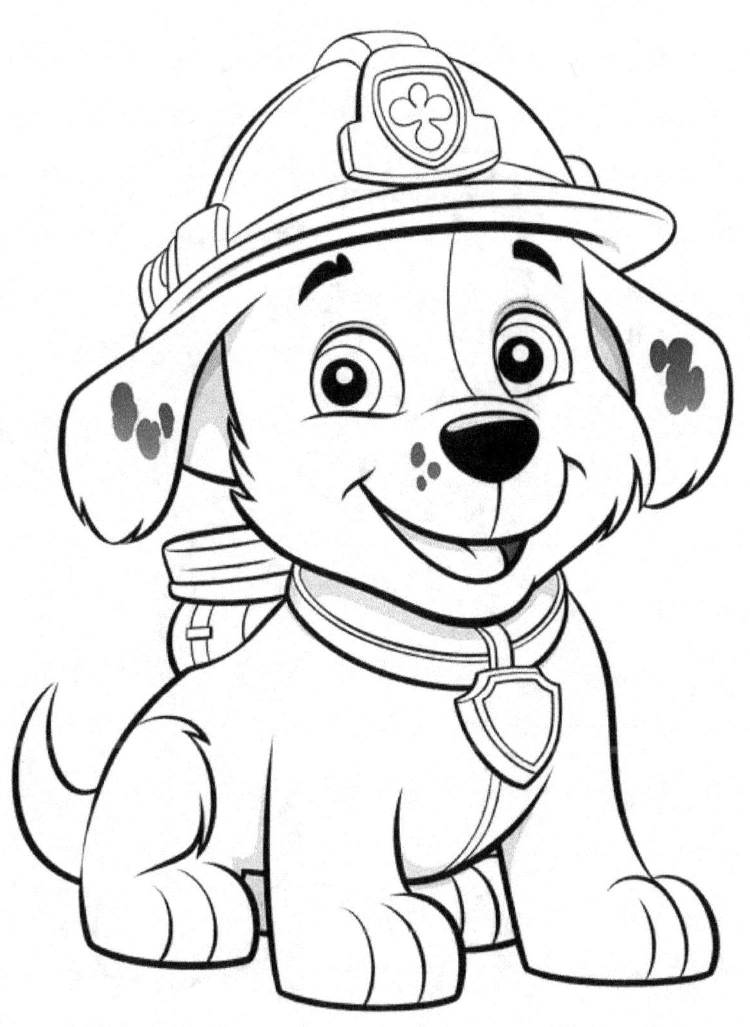

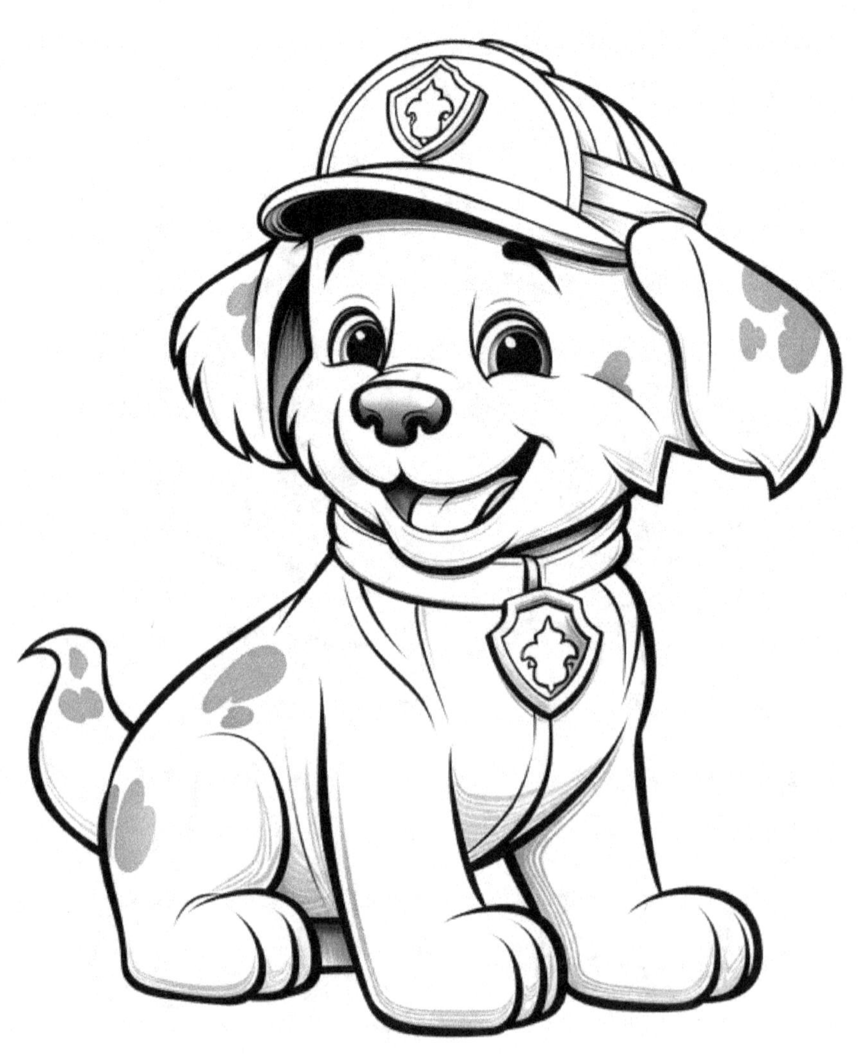

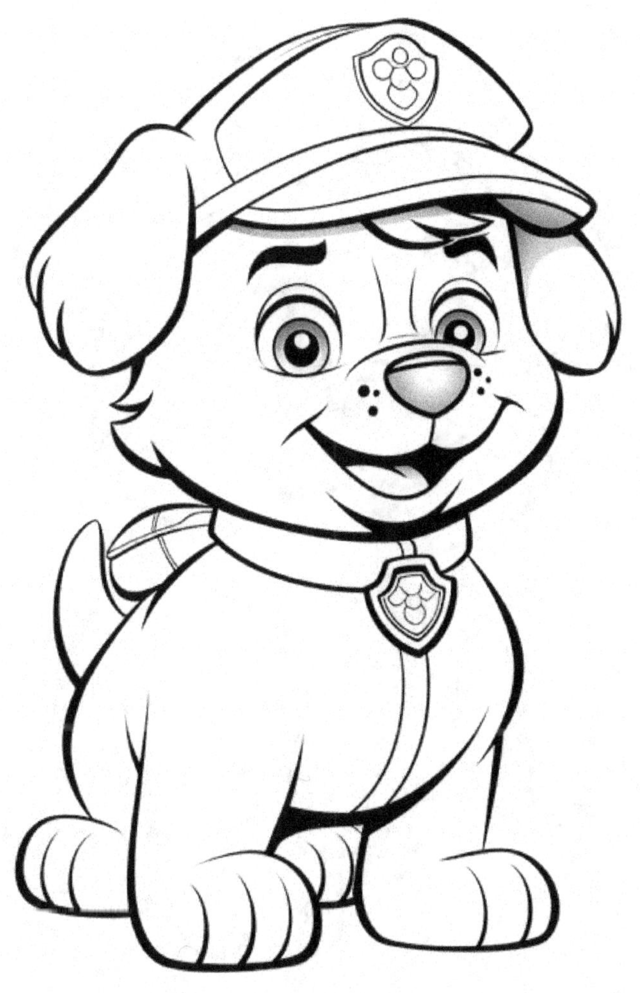

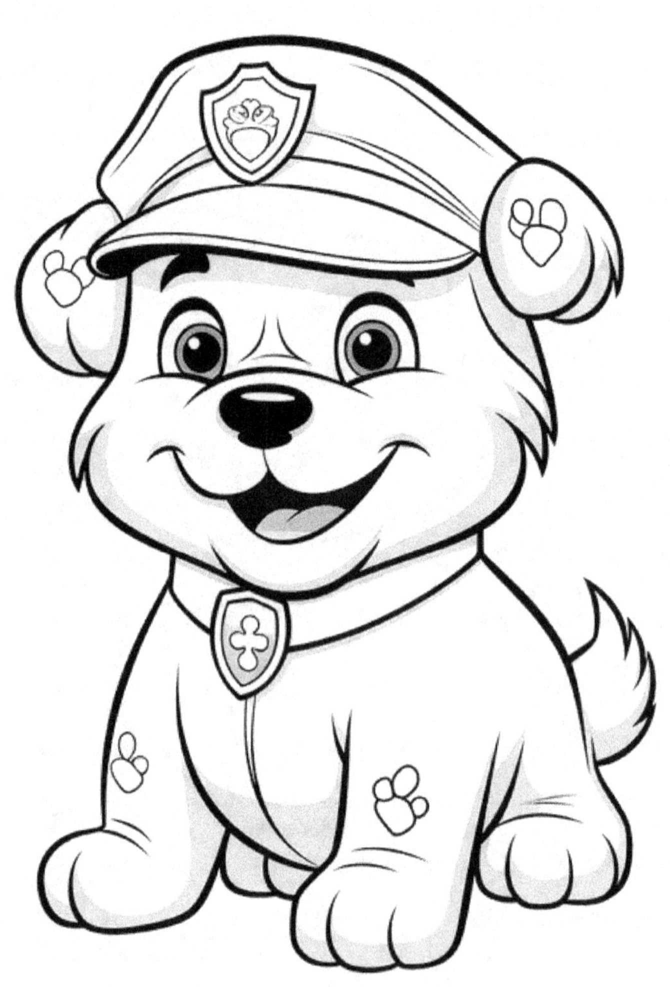

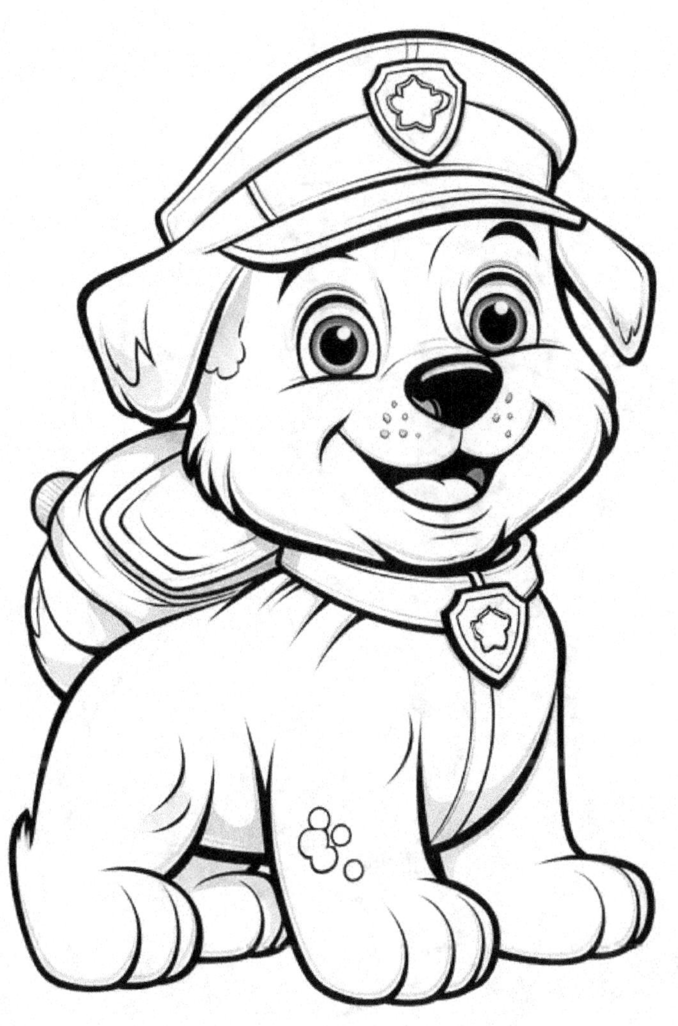

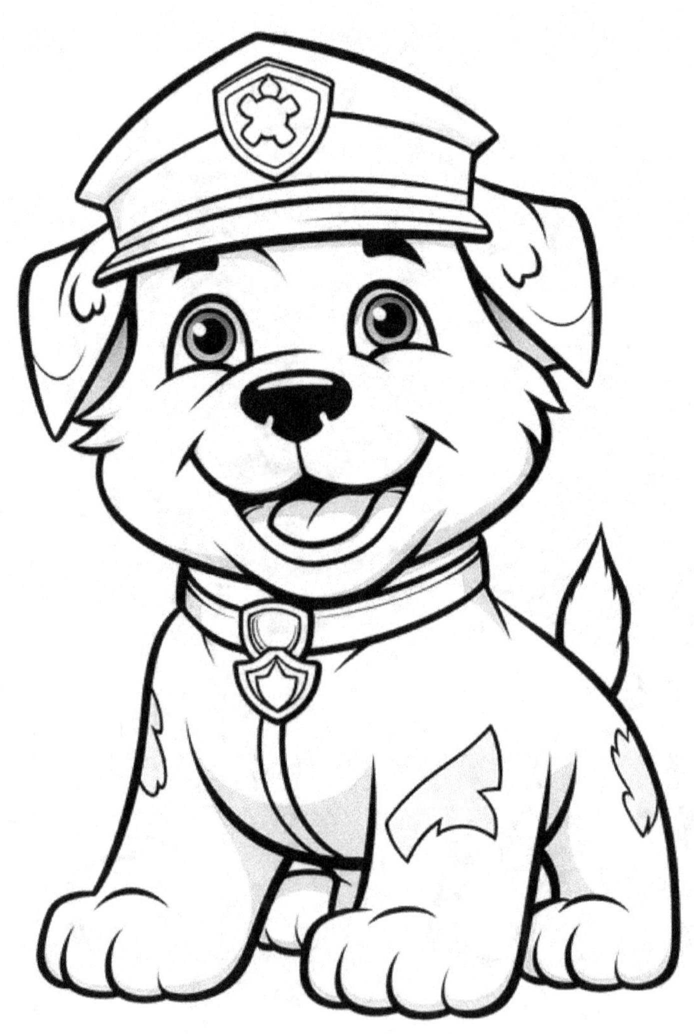

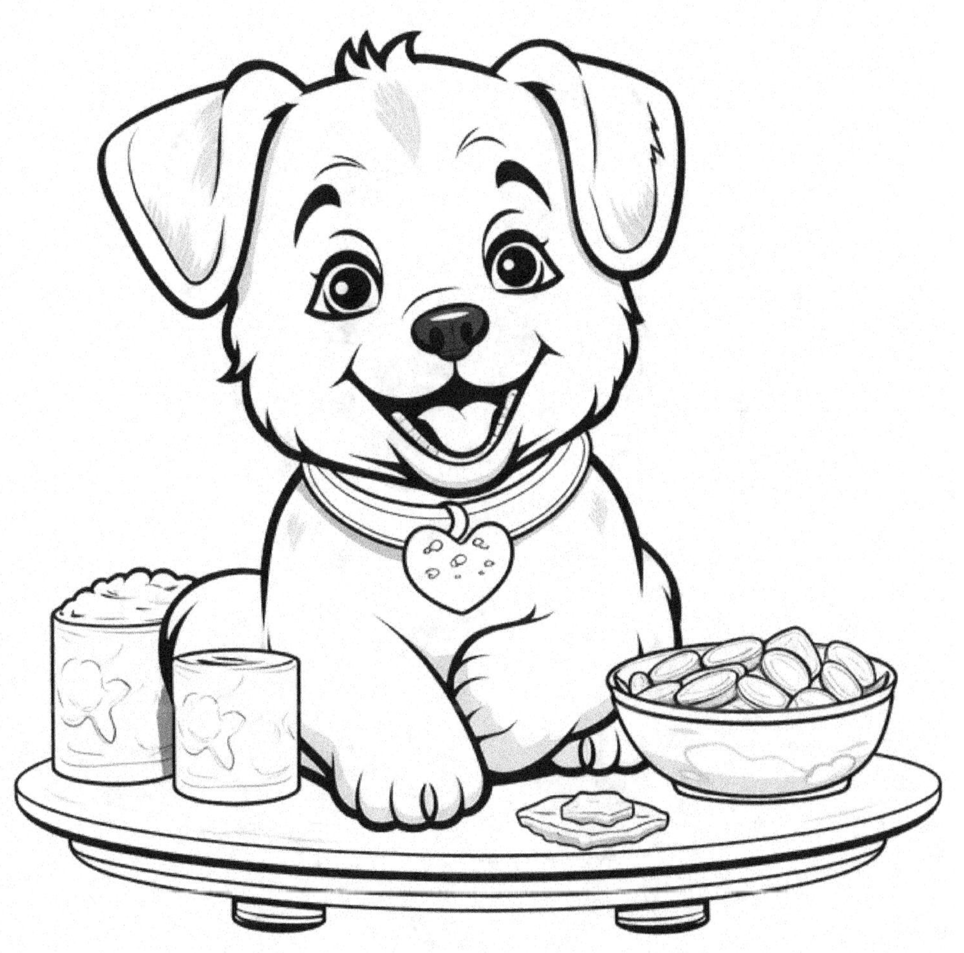

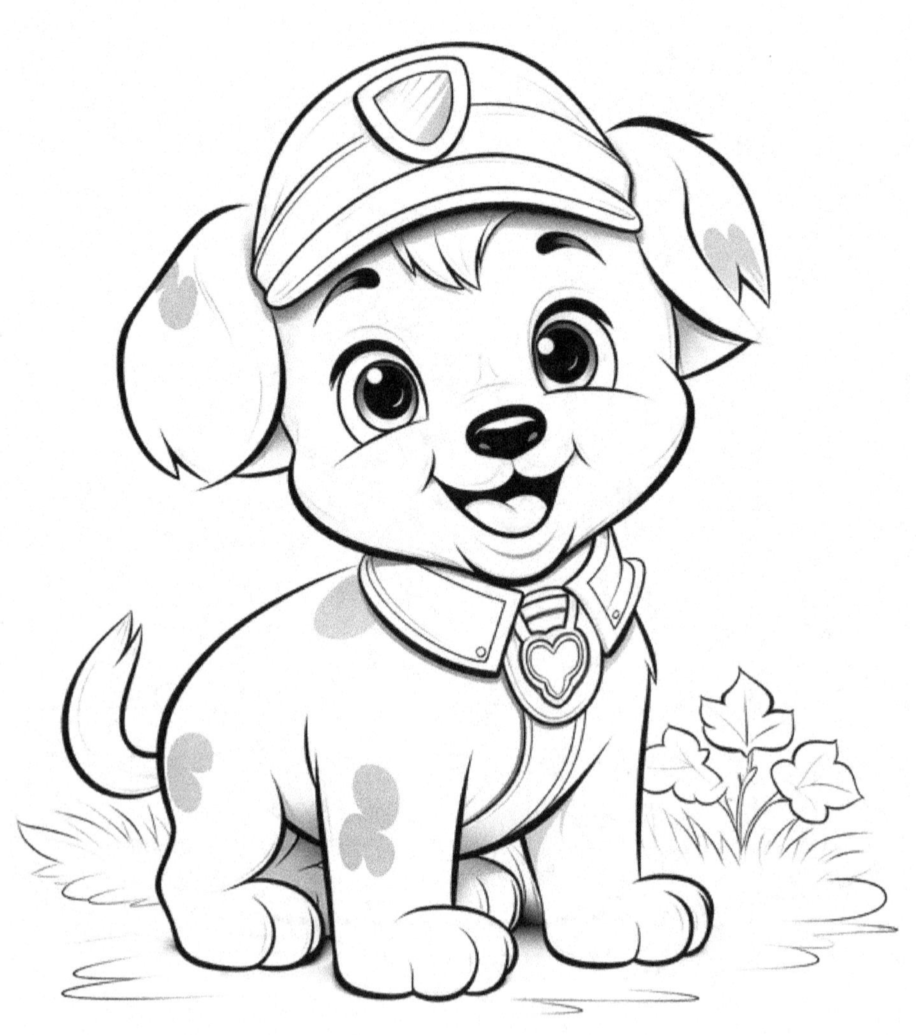

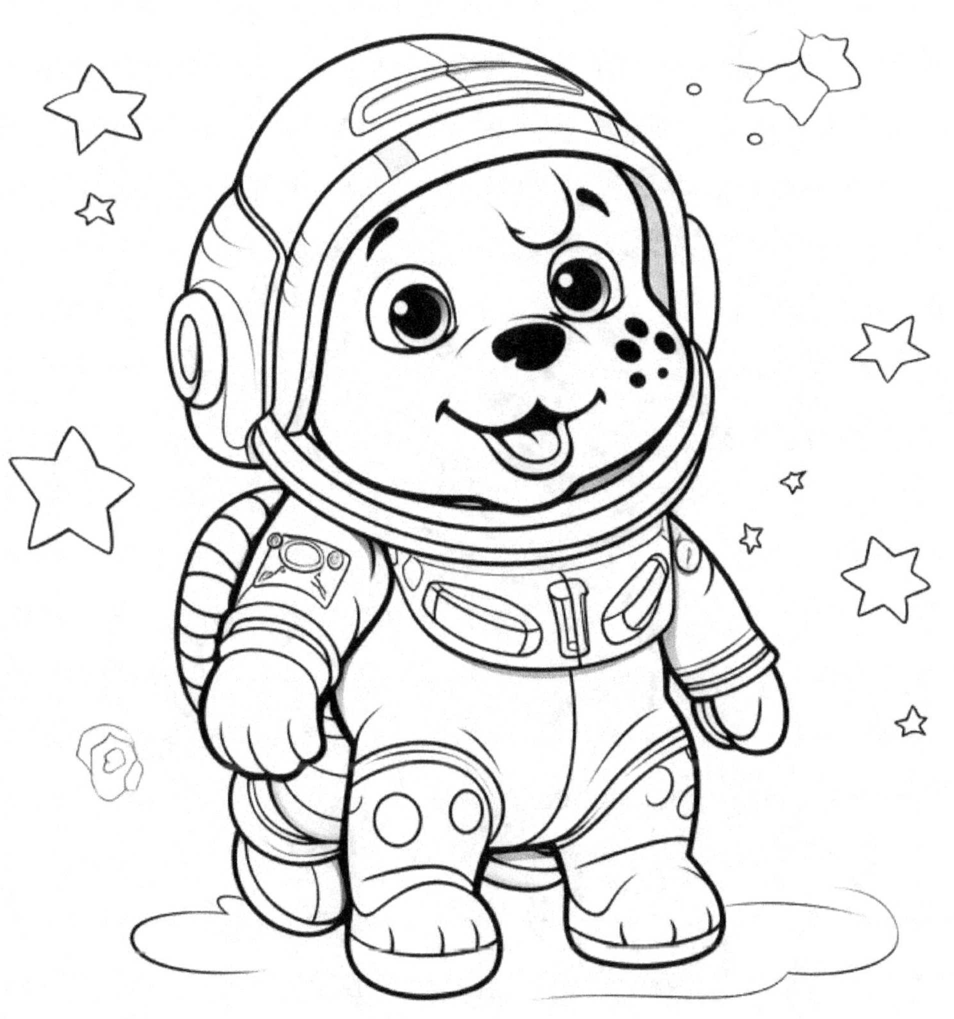

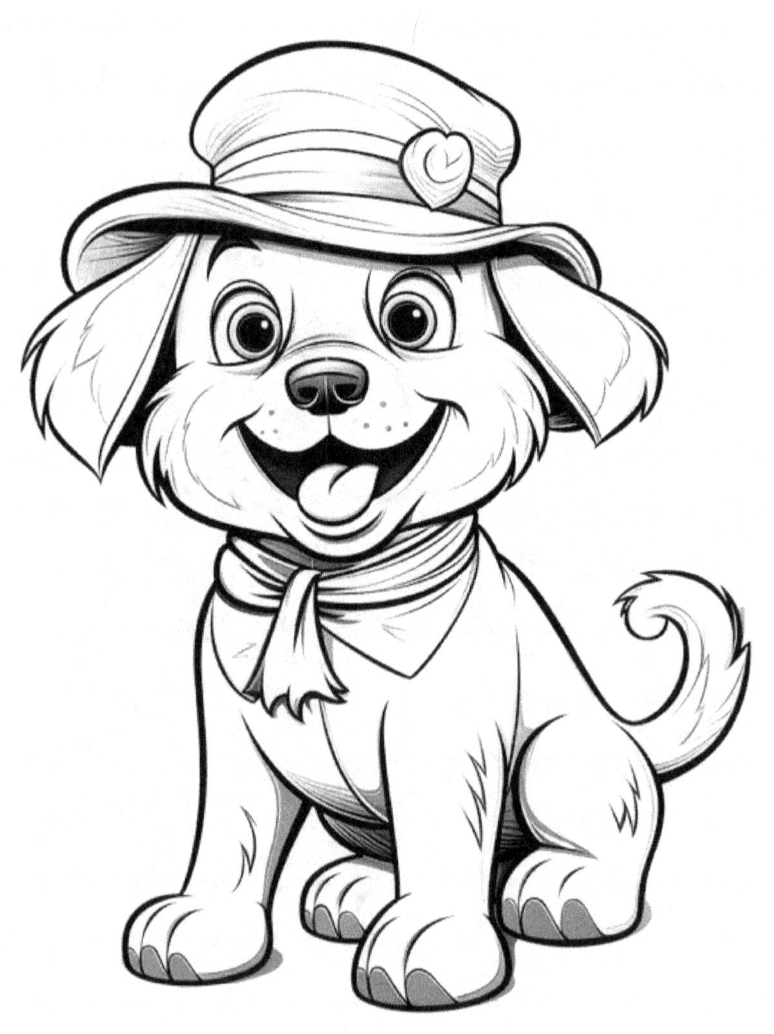

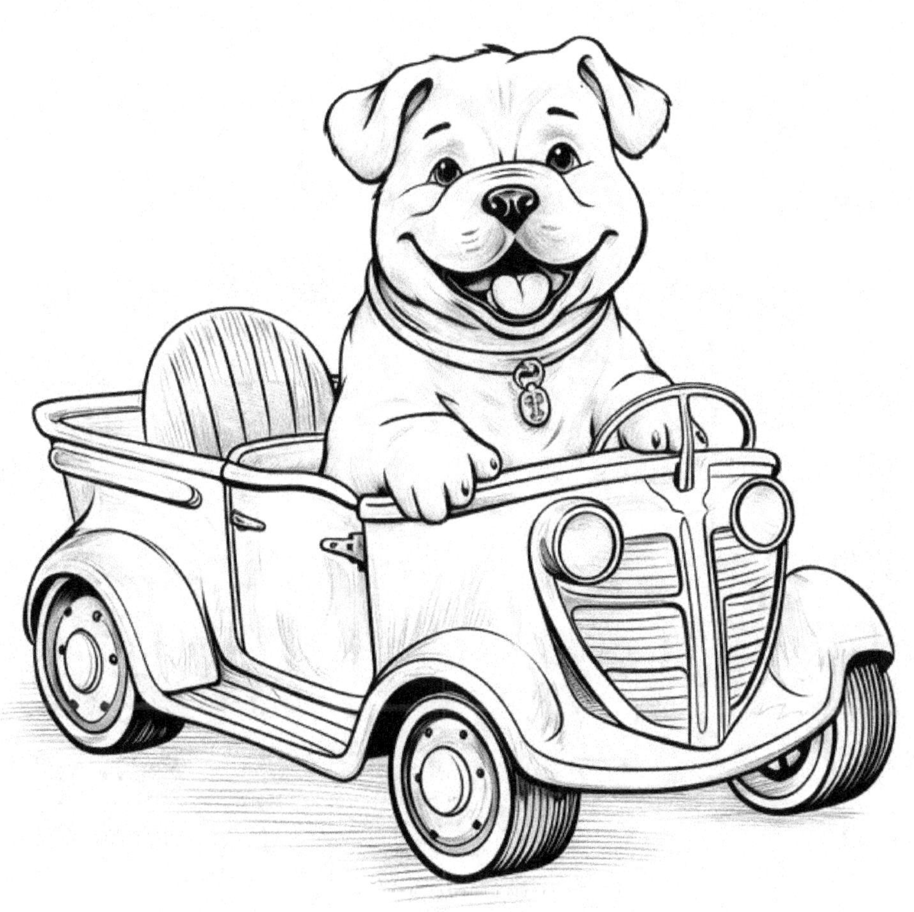

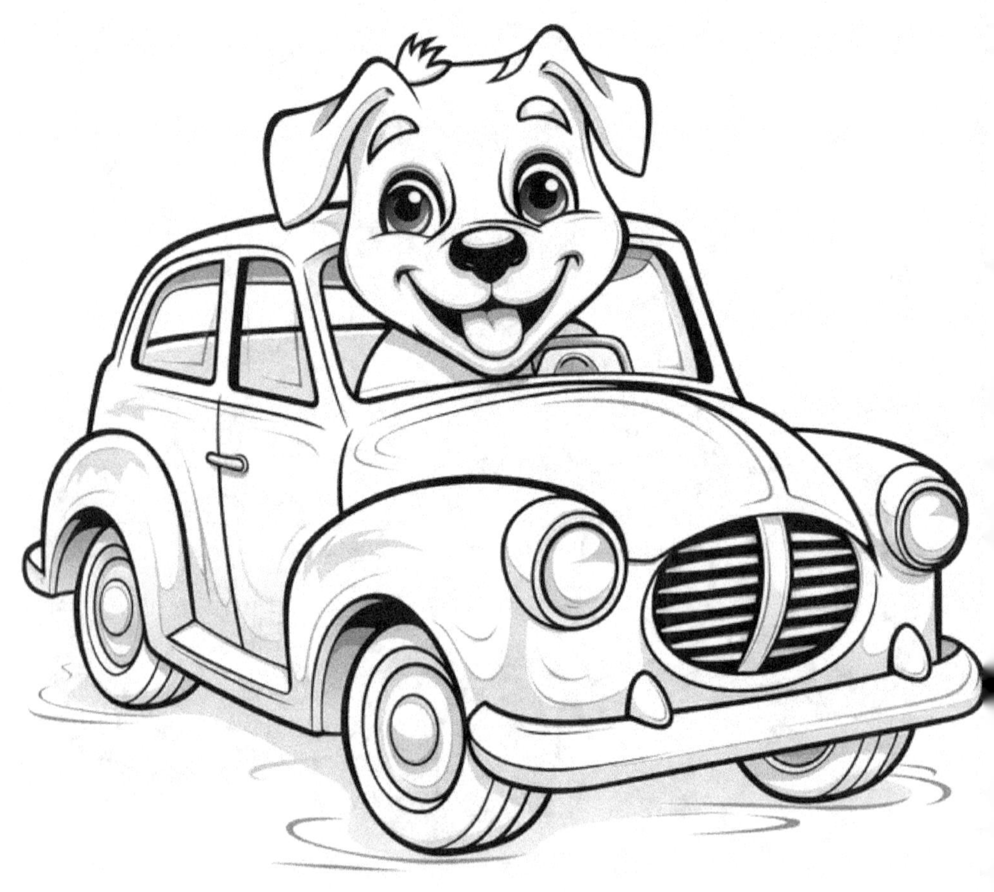

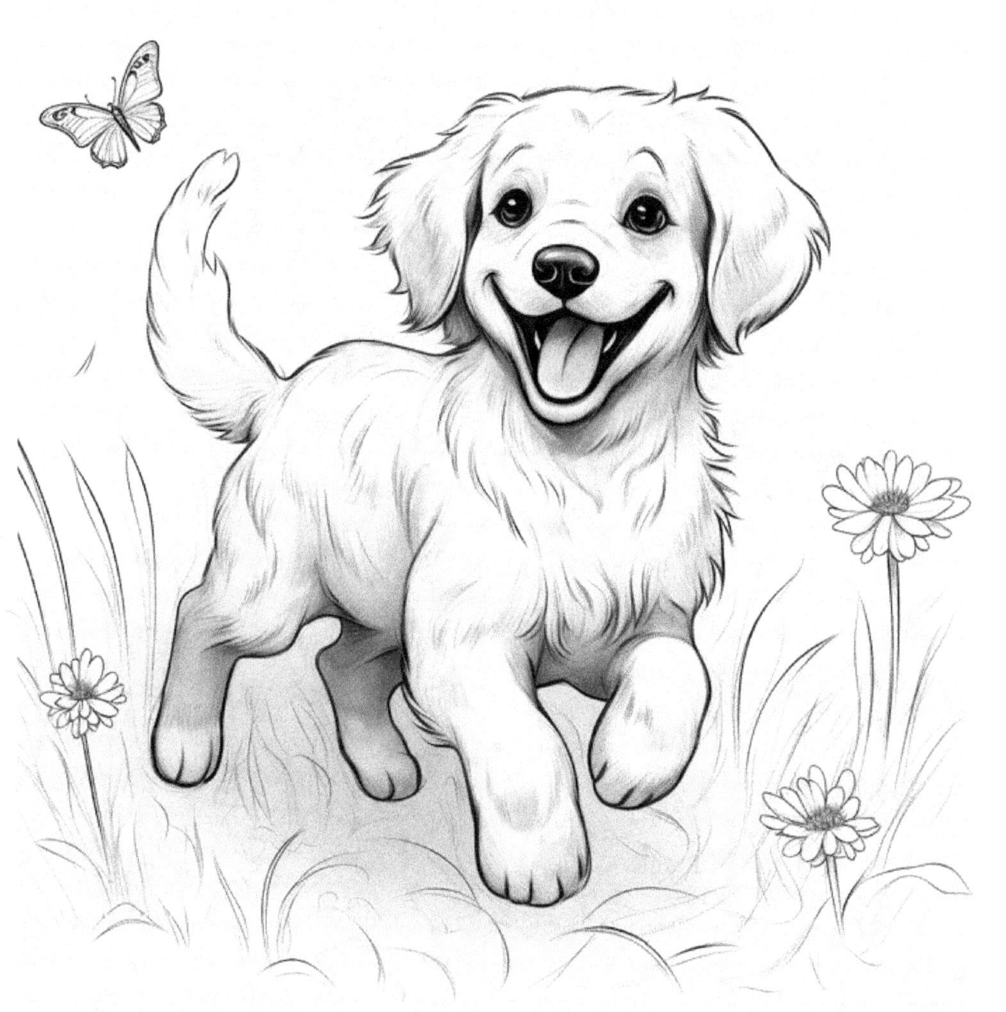

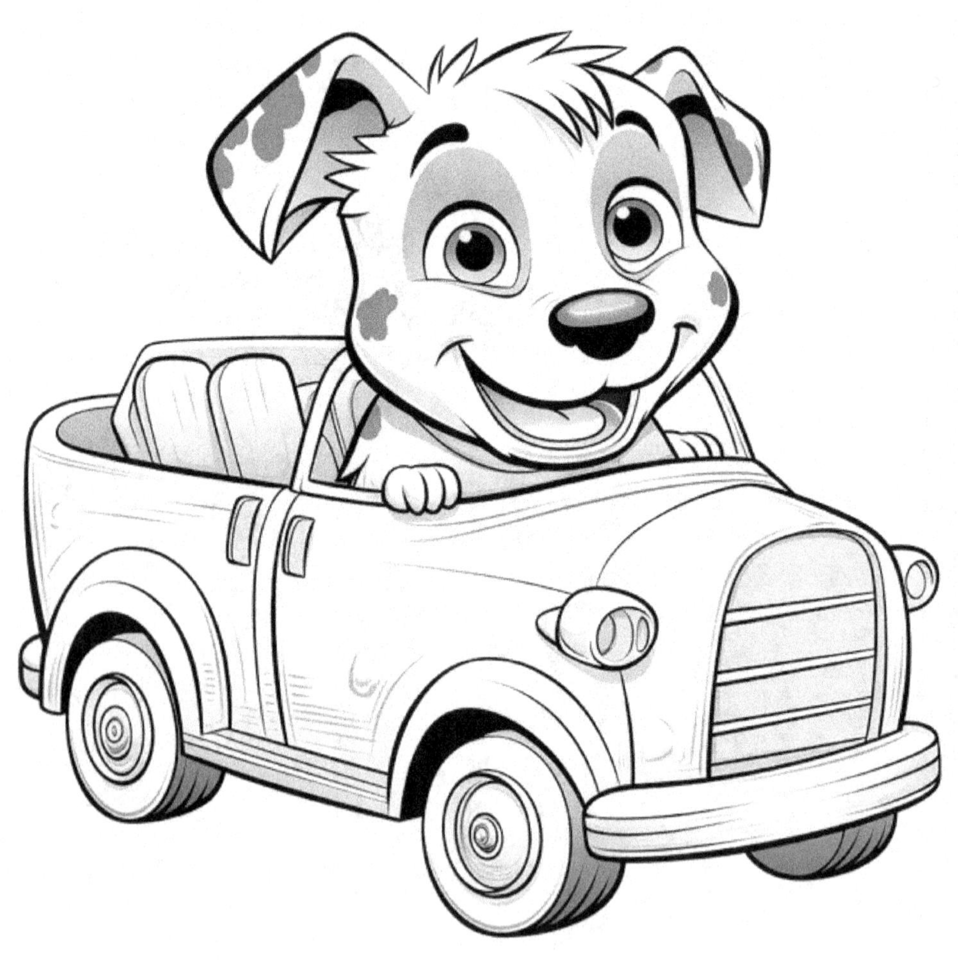

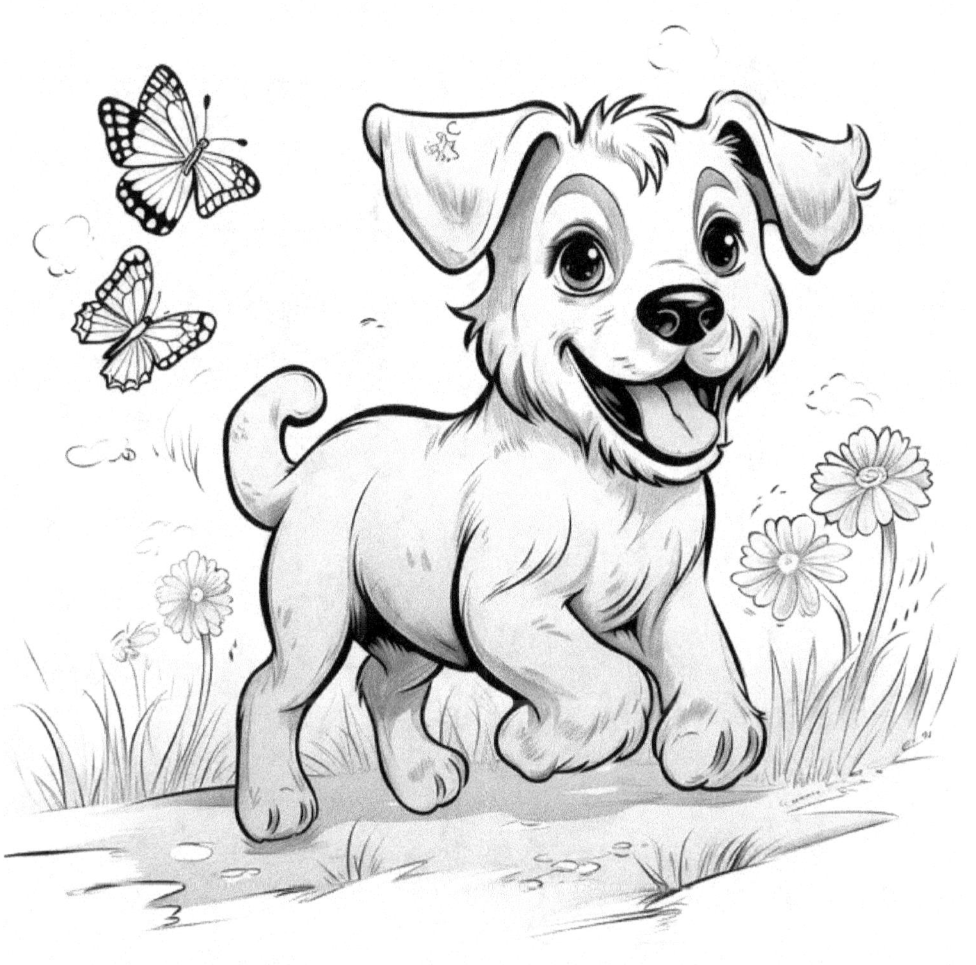

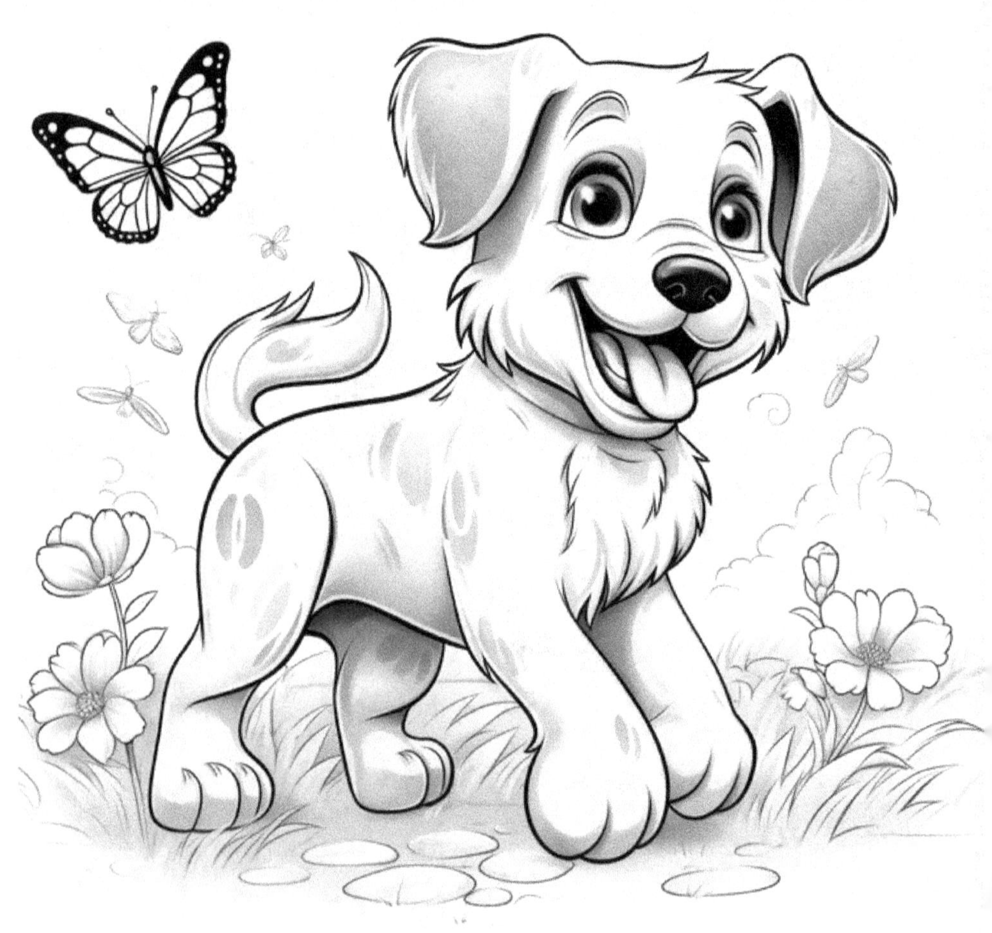

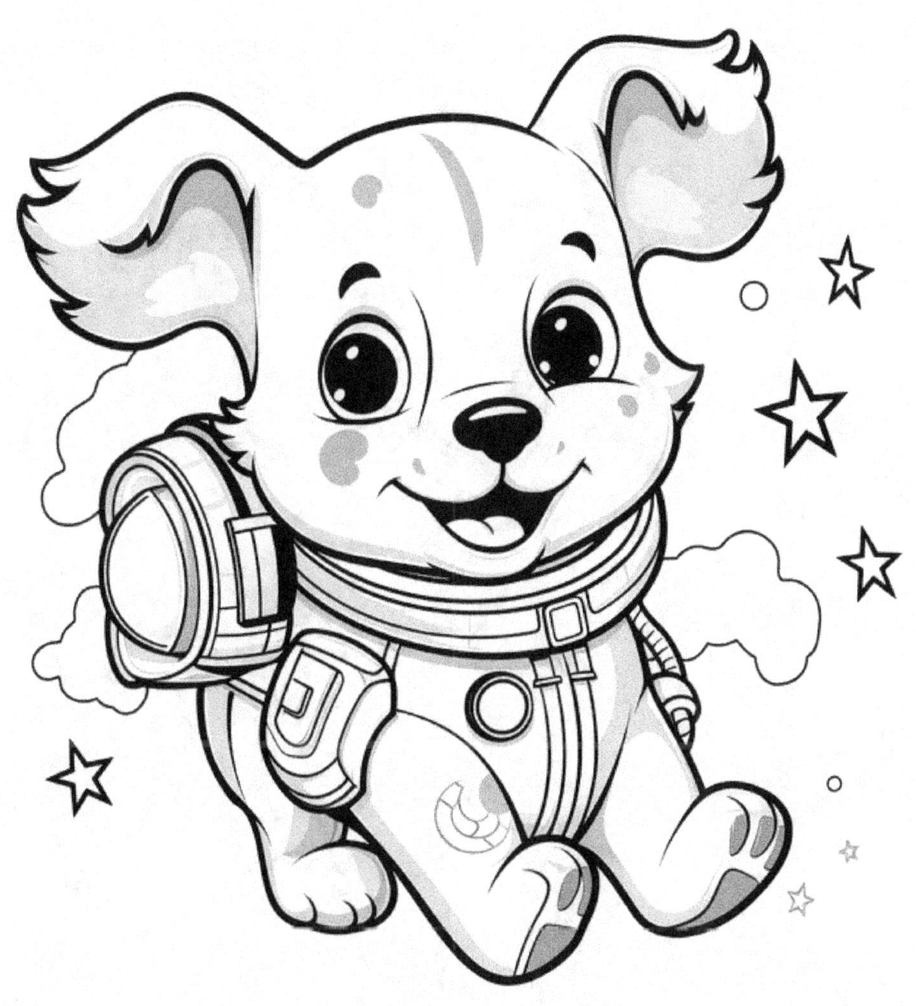

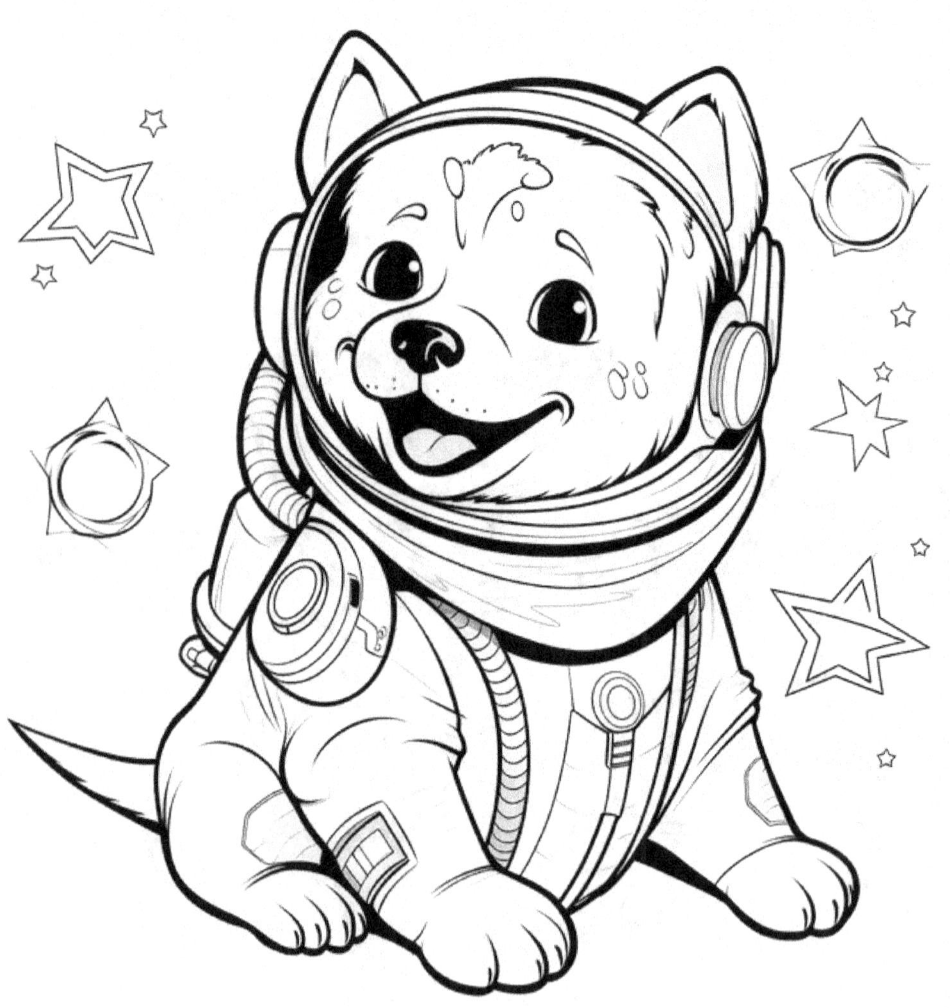

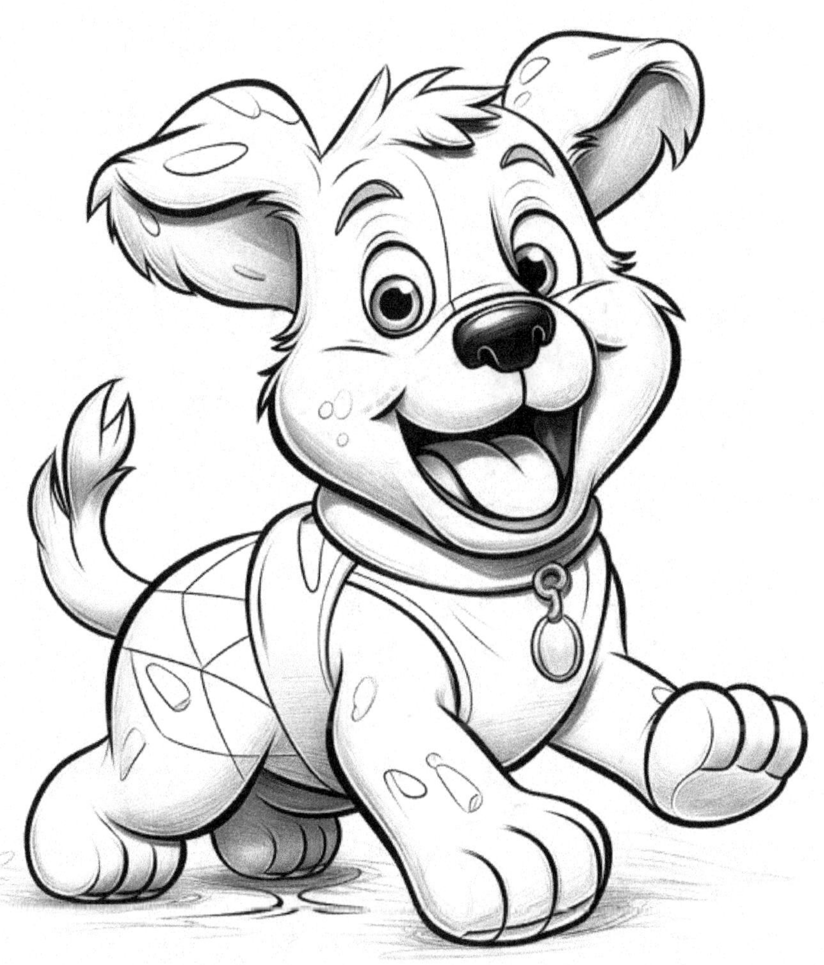

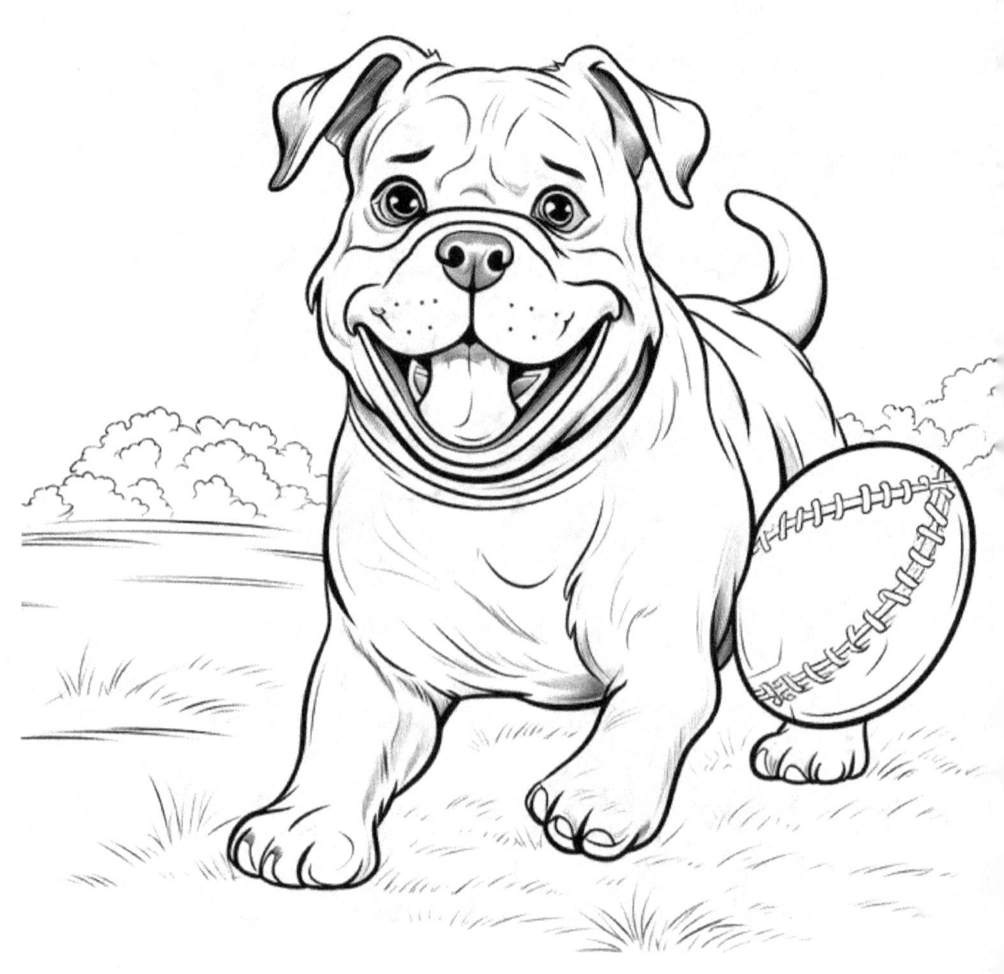

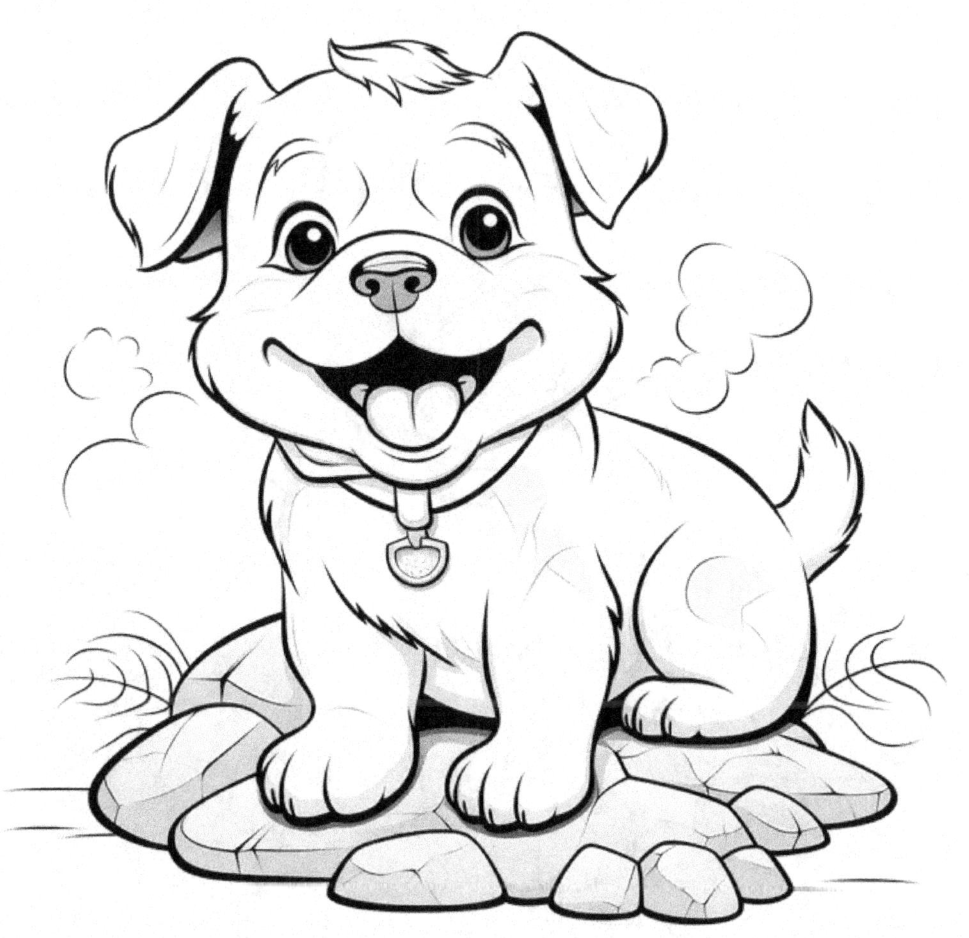

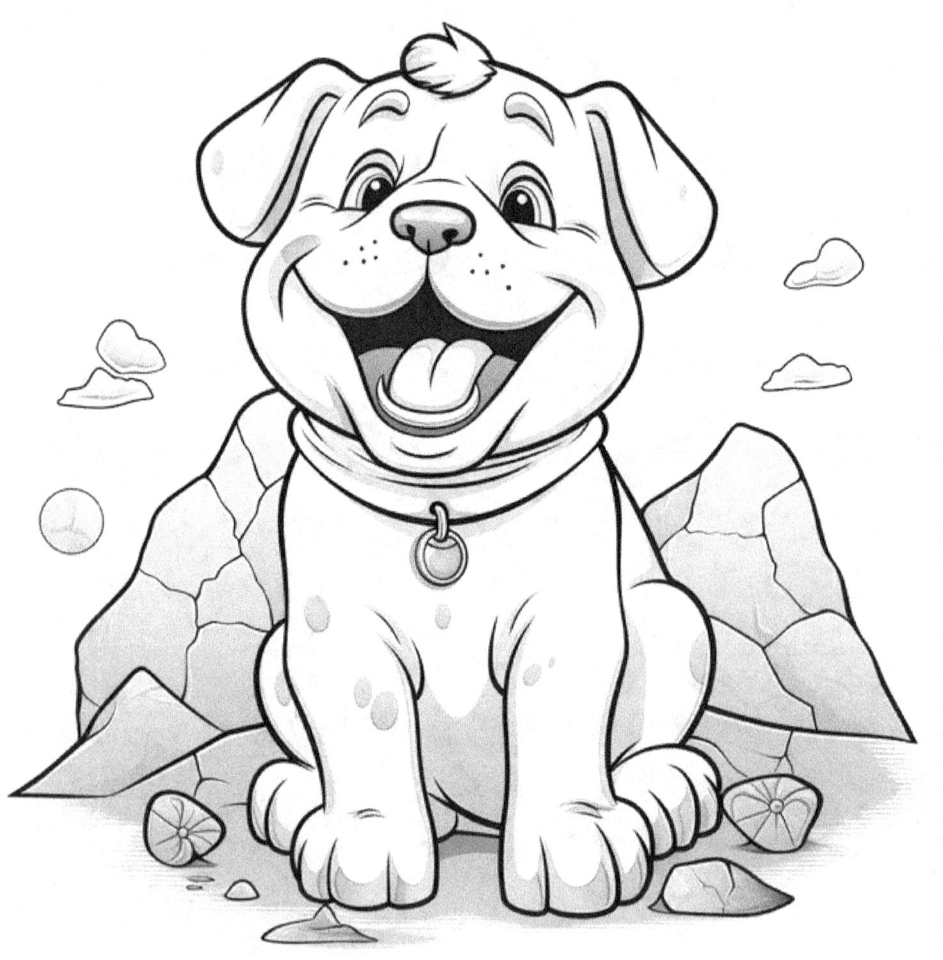

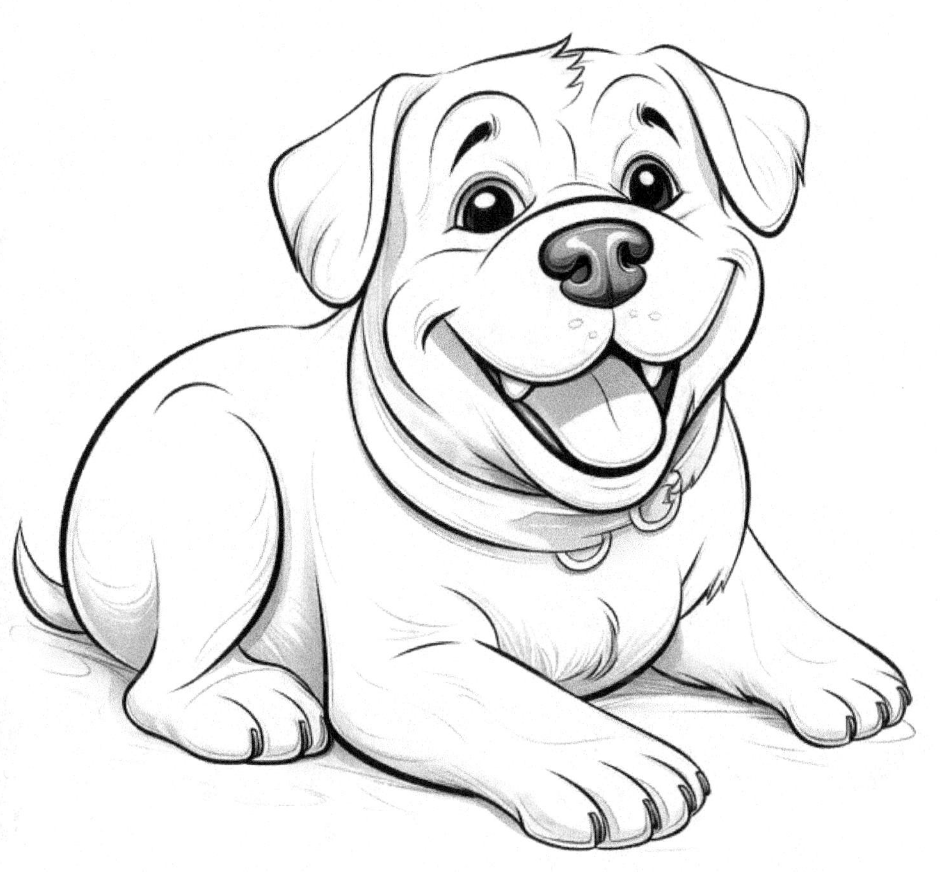

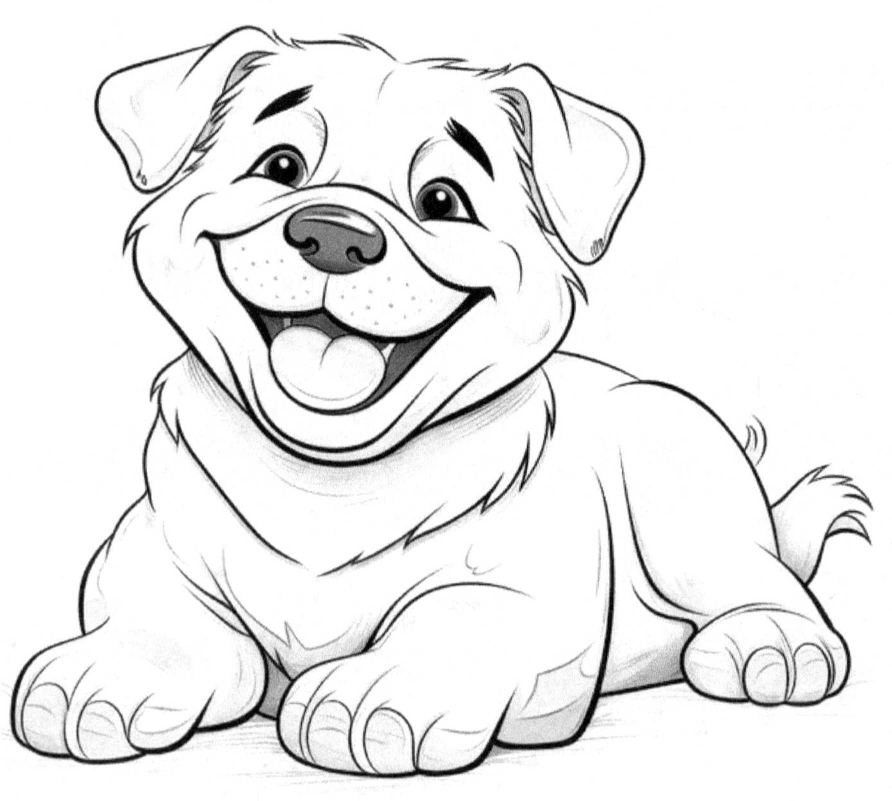

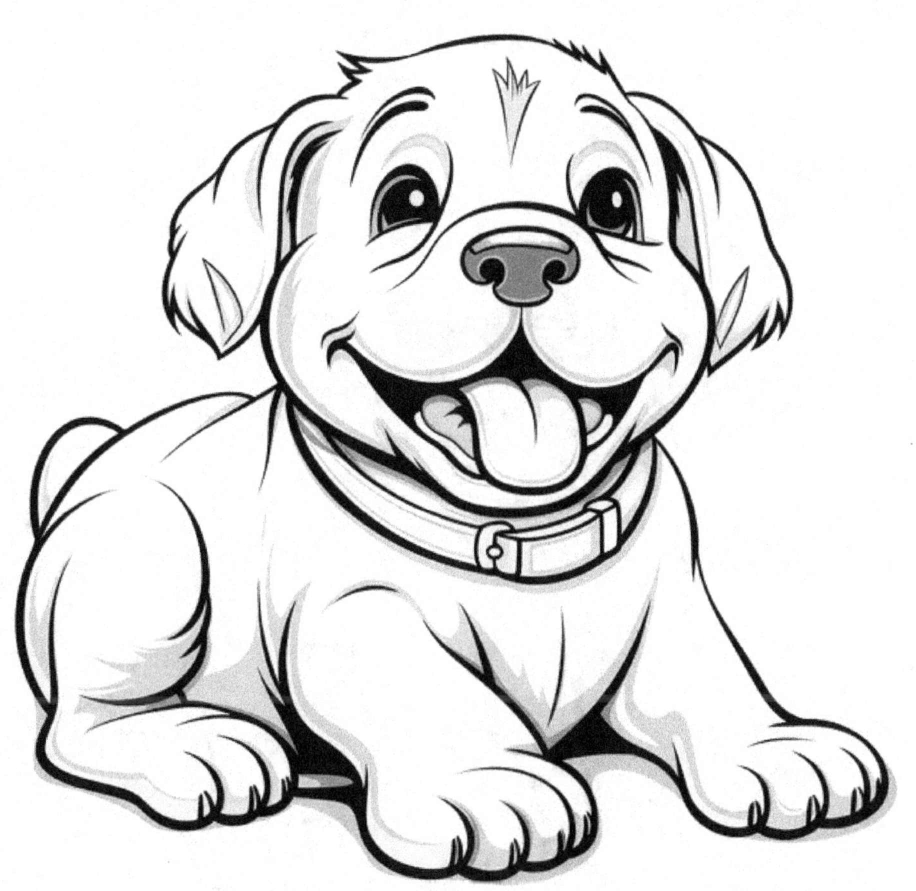

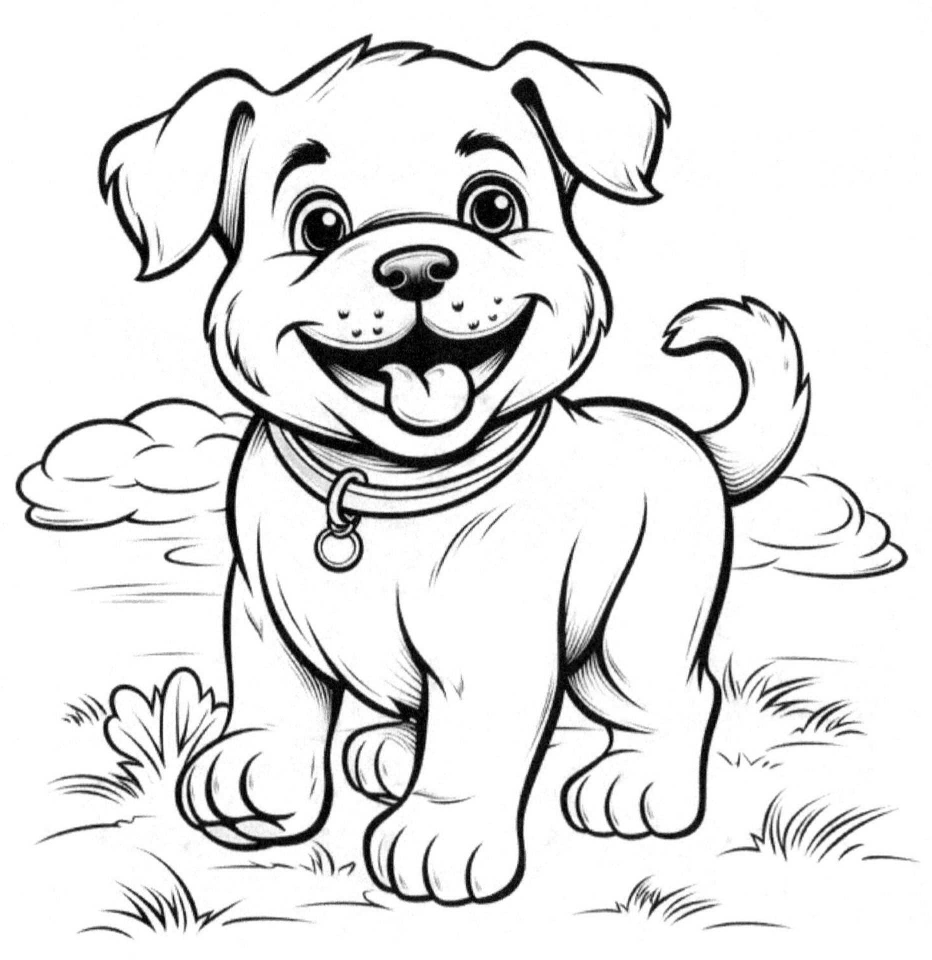

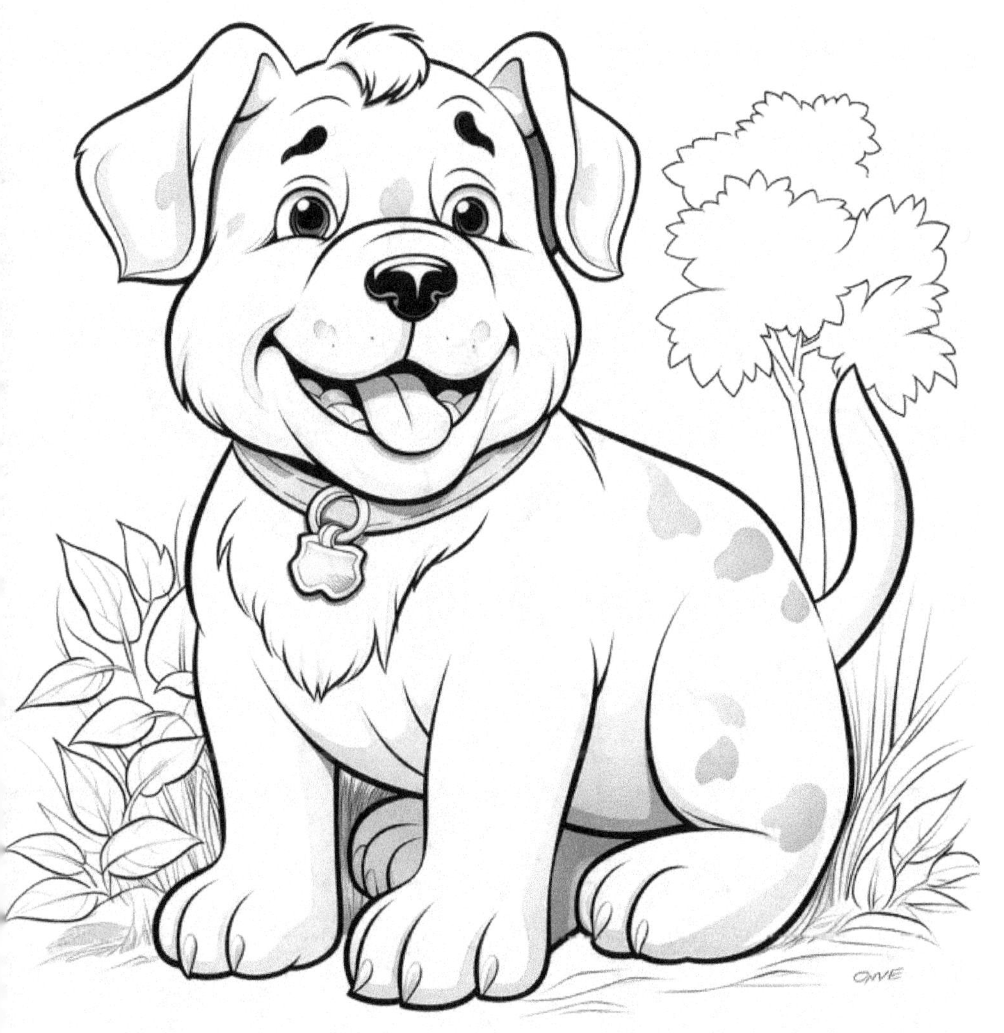

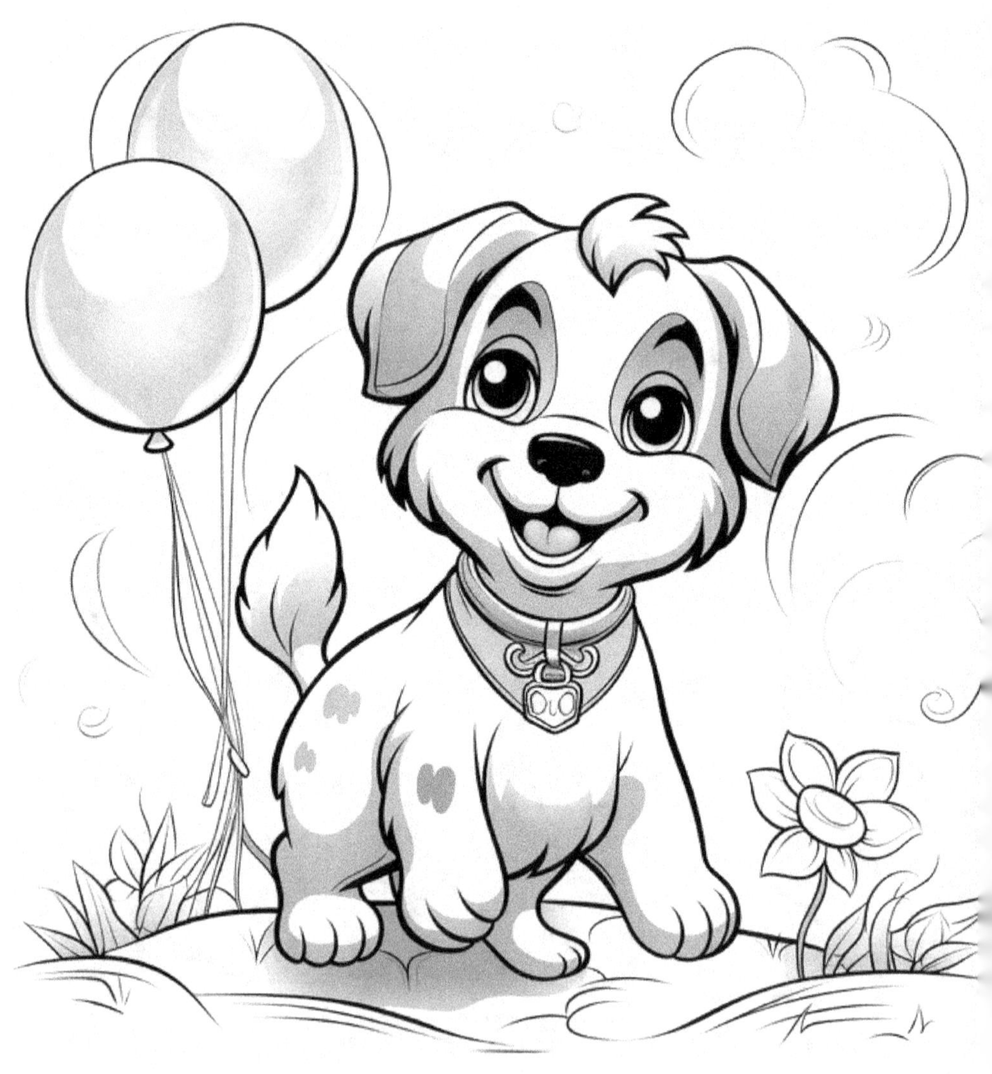

www.ingramcontent.com/pod-product-compliance
Lightning Source LLC
Chambersburg PA
CBHW070957260726
48661CB00007B/2742